"Life is like a journey across a wide ocean. On this journey, we encounter many forces that threaten our lives.... Indeed, life can be so stressful, so storm-tossed, that we fear we will be blown over the edge of safety and will drown in the turbulent sea—alone, unseen, unnoticed.

"This is a book for life's sailors, those who are brave enough to look a storm in the face and laugh above its fury. But this is also a book for those who are wise enough to know that even the saltiest sea dog needs life-rails to cling to from time to time."

Scott Walker, in the
Introduction to *Life-Rails*

Also by Scott Walker:

WHERE THE RIVERS FLOW: *Exploring the Sources of Faith Development*

DISCOVERING EXODUS: *The Guideposts Home Bible Study Program*

LIFE-RAILS

Holding Fast to God's Promises

Scott Walker

BALLANTINE BOOKS • NEW YORK

Unless otherwise noted, all Scripture quotations are from the New American Standard Bible, © The Lockman Foundation 1960, 1962, 1963, 1968, 1971, 1973, 1975, 1977, and are used by permission.

Scripture quotations marked RSV are from the Revised Standard Version of the Bible, copyrighted 1946, 1952, © 1971, 1973 by the Division of Christian Education of the National Council of the Churches of Christ in the U.S.A., and are used by permission.

Scripture quotations marked KJV are from the King James Version of the Bible.

Library of Congress Catalog Card Number: 87-10421

ISBN 0-345-35159-2

This edition published by arrangement with The Westminster Press, Publications Unit of the Presbyterian Church (U.S.A.)

Manufactured in the United States of America

First Ballantine Books/Epiphany Edition: March 1989

To my mother,
Dorothy Walker,
whose beautiful life of Christian commitment
has led me to believe in
the promises of God

ACKNOWLEDGMENTS

Many lives have contributed to the writing of this book. I would, however, particularly like to thank those special people who have allowed their stories to be shared within its pages. Their giving is immeasurable.

To Kathy Cole, Lottie Baucom, and Karen McGowan I am indebted for their skillful assistance in the preparation of this manuscript. Their patience is admirable.

Many thanks to Carlton and Carol Tyson for some wonderful days I spent in reflection and writing at their beach house.

Without the help and encouragement of Floyd Thatcher, this book would not have been published. God has given this caring man the unique gift of enabling others to dream and to write.

Finally, I have been blessed with an editor who is truly a "kindred spirit." Though we have never met in person, Mary Ruth Howes and I have walked down many roads together, and I have appreciated her professional help as well as her Christian faith.

CONTENTS

INTRODUCTION

Dreams and fantasies are a precious part of childhood. In these early formative years, there are no limits to our wide-eyed imaginations. Without the restraints of adult realism, we can at will soar through space, sail the seven seas, climb the highest mountains, and explore the most remote rivers. The dreams of childhood are vitally and refreshingly stimulating. Unfortunately, for the most part they are far removed from reality.

Once, however, when I was six, one of my wildest dreams suddenly came true. One special evening my father came home from work with some mysterious red tickets in his hand. After dinner, he and my mother shared the life-changing news with my younger sister and me. We would soon be moving to a faraway land, they told us with anxious excitement—to the Philippines—where my parents would be missionaries. The fact of becoming ''missionaries'' had little effect upon me. But when my father pulled the tickets from his pocket, set them on the table in front of my plate, and told me that we were going to sail across the Pacific on a large ocean liner, my excitement could hardly be contained. Now I really could be a sailor, a pirate, an explorer!

I never shall forget the day we drove down to the dock in San Francisco to board the S.S. *President Wilson*. The ship seemed so huge. Climbing up the narrow gangplank while clutching tightly to my father's hand, I felt as if we were climbing to the sky. We spent the rest of the afternoon on the deck, watching the large crane hoist freight down into the holds of the ship, including—much to my amazement—our new 1955 Chevrolet. For a six-year-old, it was quite an incredible day.

We were still on deck at sunset. As the sun sank into the bay, the ship began to vibrate slightly, slowly edge away from the dock, and move out to sea. While stubby tugboats nudged the gray hull, the *Wilson*'s huge propellers began to churn the water, leaving a frothing wake. Leaning against the ship's rail, we gazed at the receding shoreline, and my father began to talk quite seriously with me about safety on the high seas.

"Son," he said as he patted the varnished deck railing, "this is called a 'life-rail' and it's named that for a good reason. It can save your life. It's all that stands between you and that deep ocean out there. So don't be climbing on it or doing skin-the-cats on its rails. Because if you fall over, you'll drown."

"Daddy, if I fell over, I could swim," I quickly said. And then, sensing that what I had said was foolish, I asked, "Dad, what would really happen if I fell in the ocean?"

He was silent for a moment. Inside he was trying to decide whether I was old enough to know the horror of the truth. Finally, placing his hand on my shoulder as if to steady me, as well as to convey that this was serious business, he replied, "Son, if you fell overboard, you couldn't swim. What would happen is that you would be sucked under the ship and driven through the propellers and be instantly killed."

I was silently terrified. I had never thought of anything so horrible as being chopped up by propellers. But the calculated risk on my father's part had its desired effect. I never climbed on the life-rails. And I treated them with a respect not characteristic of a mischievous six-year-old. I might have been a holy terror in the stateroom and the dining hall, but I was most well behaved on deck.

Five years later, when I was eleven, a life-rail did truly save my life. Our family was returning to the United States on furlough, going by way of India, the Middle East, and

Europe. From London we sailed to New York on the S.S. *United States*. This stately vessel had the distinction of holding the record for the fastest transatlantic crossing. She was an impressive ship.

Partway across the Atlantic, we ran into a gale. Always fascinated by the power of storms, I wandered out on deck by myself to experience its force. The wind was blowing furiously and the whipped-up smell of salt water burned my nose. The choppy sea was as steel-gray as the plunging hull of the ship. As I walked down the long deck with the wind at my back, the gusts were so strong that they literally pushed me along. I felt like a sail being filled and propelled by a mighty breeze. On an impulse, I began to run slowly and then to sprint, exhilarated by the power of the wind thrusting me along. I was weightless, running freely and without effort. Then—I was at the stern of the ship. I could not turn, could not stop. Out of control, I crashed into the life-rail with a force that knocked the breath out of me. Nearly wrapped around the railing, I dizzily caught sight of the frothing cataract of water being churned by the ship's propellers far below, and I grew sick with terror. Had it not been for the life-rail, I would have been blown over the side of the deck to a certain death. I owed my life to a steel railing.

I have entitled this book *Life-Rails* for a specific reason. Life is like a journey across a wide ocean. On this journey, we encounter many forces that threaten our lives: waves of fear, winds of depression, powerful typhoons of anger, powerlessness, and despondency. We inevitably confront trials that are difficult to endure and decisions that are perplexing to make. Indeed, life can be so stressful, so storm-tossed, that we fear we will be blown over the edge of safety and will drown in the turbulent sea—alone, unseen, unnoticed.

But the good news is that our plunging ships do have life-rails that we can grasp and that will keep us from tumbling over the edge. These life-rails are the promises of God.

In this book I hope to place in your hands some sturdy life-rails to hold on to when you are buffeted by the storms of life. Each one is secured and bolted into the strong foundations of biblical truth. But I have painted and varnished them with the brush strokes of everyday life experiences and stories so that you may more easily lay hold of their life-saving truth.

This is a book for life's sailors, those who are brave enough to look a storm in the face and laugh above its fury. But this is also a book for those who are wise enough to know that even the saltiest sea dog needs life-rails to cling to from time to time.

Let us hold firmly to our life-rail—the eternal word of God.

WINDS OF TESTS
AND TRIALS

1

STRENGTHENED BY FIRE

As the miles flashed by and minutes merged into hours, I dreaded reaching our destination. Over and over again, I rehearsed what I might say. But every sentence that I uttered in the silence of my mind sounded hollow, inadequate, trite. What do you say to dear friends who have lost everything they own?

Beth and I had heard the news only hours before. Two of our closest friends, Johnny and Julie Knowlton, had had their home totally destroyed by fire. Fortunately, they had been on a weekend trip and their lives had been spared. But when faulty wiring in their hot water heater had erupted into flames in the middle of the night, everything in their home was reduced to ashes except what they had packed in their suitcases.

A week before the fire, Beth and I had visited with the Knowltons. Johnny had recently graduated from law school and Julie was pregnant with their first child. In a spirit of celebration and joy, they had just purchased a new piano, and we had spent some wonderful moments playing and singing together. Surrounded by the walnut and mahogany antiques that filled their living room, we had sat up talking nearly all night. Now the piano, the antiques, the newly acquired crib and nursery furniture were all gone—totally destroyed.

As we drove up the driveway to the house where the Knowltons were temporarily staying, Beth and I looked at each other with eyes full of dread. We felt like Job's friends coming from afar to bring meaningless clichés of comfort. In reality all that we could give them was our bodily presence and awkward gestures of support and love.

And yet, we soon found that words of wisdom were not needed. Johnny and Julie, although still numbed by shock, were coping with their grief much better than we had anticipated. Their faces showed the crinkled lines of fatigue and strain. And their words betrayed the fact that it would take months for the grim realities of their loss to filter through. But their attitudes were admirable. Like Job, they had refused to "curse God and die."

After a lunch of soup and sandwiches that a thoughtful Sunday school class had brought by, we decided to drive out into the countryside and view the ruins of the house. In the vain hope of discovering something of value, Johnny and I loaded shovels and rakes into the trunk of the car to dig through the rubble. We also stopped by a hardware store to buy gloves to protect our hands from the smoldering debris.

When we got to the house, I could not believe my eyes. Nothing was left. Absolutely nothing. All that was standing was part of the brick walls, scorched and twisted, looking as if they would fall at the slightest touch. Even as we gaped at the interior of the house, we realized that no amount of digging or sifting could ever recover treasured possessions. They were gone forever. We could see only the charred metal frame of the new piano. Its warped and twisted strings would never play music again.

Slowly, gingerly, we began to poke through the mounds of ashes. We tried to recall where things used to be, all the while wondering how such a large chest of drawers or canopy bed could be reduced to a few inches of soot and cinders. We had all but given up finding anything when my rake scraped against something small and blue. Brushing away the ashes Johnny recognized a little china bluebird that had sat on top of a chest in the living room.

I picked it up and began to wipe away the soot. It was completely intact and its colors were still bright. Except for a few hairline cracks in the glaze, it had survived the intense heat in fine condition. We were astounded.

After sifting through the ashes for another hour or so, we recovered only a pair of brass candlesticks and a ceramic vase from Korea. Giving up on further salvaging, we began our return to the apartment, a china bluebird, brass candlesticks, and a ceramic vase the only survivors of their life's possessions.

In the car I carefully cradled the little bluebird in my hands and tried to wipe the remaining smudges away. As I gazed down at the bird's small beak and two black eyes, I wanted to weep. If only this little bluebird could talk, what a story it would tell! A story of the heat of the night, of terror, of survival against great odds. And then the crucial question hit me. Why did this china bluebird survive? Why were two brass candlesticks and a ceramic vase not destroyed when a piano, an antique bed, classical records, and wedding pictures did not make it through the holocaust to see another day? The bluebird was silent, but I sensed that between my hands I held the answer to some of life's most difficult questions.

We drove home through a bleak winter's landscape, past stark and leafless pecan trees silhouetted against a golden sunset sky. Slowly, an answer to my question began to filter into my awareness. In the dimness of the car, I felt the glazed smoothness of the little bird and realized that it had survived the fire because it had been tested by fire before. Both the china bird and the ceramic vase had endured because long before this fire, they had been baked in flaming kilns and the kilns had tempered them so they could survive a future fire. So, too, the brass candlesticks. In years past the raw metal had been brought up from the depths of the earth, had been melted and refined and cast. Because of this refining process the candlesticks had withstood the fiery test, while the wax candles had melted away and the wooden chest on which they rested had been reduced to cinders and ashes.

I looked at Johnny and Julie, their faces now softened in the shadows of dusk and the rise of a crescent moon. Though singed, they, too, had survived this fire and would continue to surmount other crises in life. The ordeal of the fire would force them to mature and would enable them to remain true and firm in the wilting heat of future years when others burned out and hopes turned to ashes.

As darkness finally captured the earth and our headlights shone down the highway, my thoughts turned to the novel I had been reading recently, *A Farewell to Arms* by Ernest Hemingway. In this powerful work Hemingway had said, "The world breaks every one and afterward many are strong at the broken places."[1] I sensed he was right. Strength does often come from brokenness, from the salt of tears, from trials and tribulations.

Then from the Bible, the word of God, the voice of James the brother of Jesus came flashing across the centuries. Toward the end of his life, after struggling to lead the Jerusalem Church through years of turmoil, he had faced his own certain persecution and said:

> Consider it all joy, my brethren, when you encounter various trials, knowing that the testing of your faith produces endurance. And let endurance have its perfect result, that you may be perfect and complete, lacking in nothing (James 1:2–4).

We in the car that evening didn't feel joyful or perfect or complete. But the message was clear. Even in the midst of the ashes of tragedy and pain, a victory can be salvaged—joints can be made stronger, minds may grow wiser, and a faith may be burned deeper by the refining fires of life.

ⅢⅢ REFLECTIONS ⅢⅢ

"And it will come about in all the land,"
Declares the Lord,
"That two parts in it will be cut off and perish;
But the third will be left in it.
And I will bring the third part through the fire,
Refine them as silver is refined,
And test them as gold is tested.
They will call on My name,

And I will answer them;
I will say, 'They are My people,'
And they will say, 'The Lord is my God.' "

Zechariah 13:8–9

We also exult in our tribulations, knowing that tribulation brings about perseverance; and perseverance, proven character; and proven character, hope; and hope does not disappoint, because the love of God has been poured out within our hearts through the Holy Spirit who was given to us.

Romans 5:3–5

Therefore we do not lose heart, but though our outer man is decaying, yet our inner man is being renewed day by day. For momentary, light affliction is producing for us an eternal weight of glory far beyond all comparison.

2 Corinthians 4:16–17

It has done me good to be somewhat parched by the heat and drenched by the rain of life.

Henry Wadsworth Longfellow[2]

As sure as even God puts his children in the furnace he will be in the furnace with them.

Charles H. Spurgeon[3]

It is the crushed grape that yields the wine.

Anonymous

DEAR GOD:

It is hard for me to thank You today for the tragedies and heartaches I have encountered in my life. It is hard for me to thank You because I know that You didn't bestow the tragedies upon me—You didn't will them, nor want them, nor cause them. They just happened. And I refuse to blame You for them.

But Father, I do want to thank You for being there with me when I cried and shook and asked, "Why me?" There were times I felt empty—when I reached for You and couldn't find You. And yet I know You were there. Thank You for the courage You have given me to face another day and try again.

Yet more than anything else, I want to thank You, Father, for using my trials to strengthen me, to make me wiser, to cause me to be more empathetic to the struggles of others. O Lord, take my crucifixions and slowly, over time, turn them into resurrections, through Jesus Christ, my Lord.

AMEN

2

FLOWERS THAT BLOOM

Approaching the family waiting room on the surgical floor of the hospital, I tried to ignore the tightening knot in my stomach and instead to exude an air of cheery confidence. As I entered the door, a dozen faces riveted tensely upon me to see if I were the bearer of news concerning the outcome of the surgery of their wife or child or loved one. Disappointed that I was not a surgeon, their eyes returned to stare at their newspapers, coffee cups, or simply at their feet. The anxiety level in a surgical waiting room is always sky high.

Scanning the room, I saw Bill Hale sitting in a corner, gazing out the window. Twenty-five years my senior, he was, nonetheless, one of my dearest friends, and I wanted to be with him during this time. His wife, Helen, was undergoing surgery with no expectation of complications, yet you never know. There is no such thing as minor surgery when a loved one faces the scalpel.

Plopping down next to Bill, I tried to be appropriately sober and yet lighthearted. I wanted to be buoyant and help him float on the waves of this crisis. After fifteen minutes of diversionary talk, however, it became increasingly hard not to speak of the gravity of the situation at hand.

Finally, I said to Bill, "It surely would be nice to have a stressless life, wouldn't it?" Bill smiled and turned to look out the window. In the brief silence that followed, pictures of Bill's and Helen's lives flashed before my eyes. . . .

*   *   *

They were both the children of parents who, during the Depression, worked long and hard hours in the textile mills of the deep South. Life had been hand-to-mouth—at times rugged—but filled with the simple pleasures of which a later generation would be deprived. Time revolved around the mill whistle and the weary shuffling of feet as work shifts changed. And there was always work! The looms of the mill never ceased their motion except on Christmas Day.

And yet, their work-enslaved parents, who had little thought of opportunities for themselves, made sure that their children had the privilege of attending school. They clearly perceived that education was the passport to a better world. And they desperately wanted their children to make that journey.

It was in high school that Bill met Helen. Their relationship was one that simply had to be. He was the cocky drum major in the band, she, a leggy majorette. And between brassy notes, whirling batons, and the busy cadence of marching feet, they began a romance that never dimmed.

Still, their relationship was not without its struggles. Immediately after his high school graduation in 1944, Bill was inducted into the army and sent to the war in the Pacific. He had missed the battles of Guadalcanal, Leyte, Saipan. But the greatest assault lay ahead—the invasion of Japan. Over a million American casualties were anticipated.

As Bill waited for the invasion aboard a crowded troopship steaming toward Japan, the most important moment of the day became the mail call. Each day's letters spoke of wedding plans, future dreams, and a better world when the war ended. But between the lines were unspoken words of fear—the fear of Bill's death, the anxiety of separation, the panic of being gripped and shaken by forces they could not control. These were stressful days.

And then, suddenly, with a shearing blast of light and the rise of mushroom clouds over Hiroshima and Nagasaki, the war was over. Troopships changed course from Tokyo to San Francisco. Bill returned to South Carolina, to Helen, to marriage, to a honeymoon in Atlanta, and, finally, to Furman

University. Life was suddenly full and promising. The belligerent fist of war and suffering had released its deadly grip.

Even with the funds for college available through the G.I. Bill, however, there was not enough money to make ends meet. Helen worked as a secretary during the day while Bill attended classes. When the last lecture note was scribbled, he would rush to catch the trolley to the textile mills to work the four-to-twelve shift. At midnight, he would walk home to study briefly before going to bed. Life was promising.

Three years later, after graduation, Bill began teaching in a South Carolina high school. A short time later he was given the chance of a lifetime—he was asked to become the school's principal. Jumping at the opportunity, he became the youngest principal in the state. Bill found the job and the young people challenging and he and Helen both grew to be dearly loved by the community and students. They had found their niche. The clatter of the textile looms was now only a memory.

During those years, Helen gave birth to a daughter and, later, a son. They were beautiful children who not only gave their young parents pleasure but also bonded them together in a way they could not have experienced before. Yet more than just children were being born into the Hale family. A dream, as well, was incubating and demanding birth.

One day while at a principals' meeting, a visiting professor from Florida State University walked up to Bill and asked, "Hale, have you ever thought about getting your doctorate? If you haven't, you should." Bill dismissed the idea as impractical, but the dream had been conceived. A year later, he resigned his position, packed up the family, and moved to Tallahassee, Florida, to attend Florida State University. It was a move of total faith.

Years later, he laughed as he commented, "I bought my first notebook and prominently wrote on its cover 'Desertation' only to cringe when I realized I had misspelled the word." There were many days and nights when Bill wondered whether he had misspelled far more than a word on a notebook—whether it had been a mistake to leave a secure job, uproot a family, expose himself to a new challenge and the possibility of failure. In the end, however, he learned to spell "dissertation" and graduated with honors and self-respect.

Rather than returning to South Carolina, Bill took a job with the University of Georgia. A vastly creative person, he became the director of the educational television division. Amidst a community of professors, producers, and artists, Bill was inspired to continue to grow and expand intellectually and philosophically. However, an event soon transpired that engendered a greater insight into life—a greater search for meaning and understanding—than any other experience in his life.

With the rigors of graduate school behind them, Bill and Helen decided to complete their family with one last child. When Kathy was born, there was a great sense of wholeness and joy. The family was secure, their roots in a new community were growing deep, and this new, awe-inspiring baby symbolized the miracle of life.

As Kathy grew, the center of her family's love and attention, gradually Bill and Helen began to sense that something was wrong. It became increasingly apparent that Kathy was having difficulty mastering certain skills, and after extensive testing, she was diagnosed as having serious learning disabilities. Somehow segments of the intricate network of the brain had not developed correctly and mental messages were being short-circuited. Although not mentally retarded, Kathy would never be able to function fully in life without special training, support, and large doses of love and understanding.

Bill and Helen were brokenhearted. What was nearly unbearable was the realization that Kathy's situation could not be "fixed." No amount of work, resolve, or money could repair this condition. They could only love her, encourage her, and see that she received the best therapeutic help possible. Grieved—though not destroyed—they determined to spend a lifetime helping Kathy reach her fullest potential.

For her first schooling they enrolled her in an excellent private school. Although no one knew how far she could advance, most of her teachers did not envision high school as a future option for her. Somewhere in elementary school, they said, she would reach the limits of her ability. Yet now—some eighteen years later—Kathy was one month away from receiving a high school certificate! With all the love and support of her family, she had beaten the odds. Although still not able to read as she should, she had shown remarkable abilities in the areas of . . .

Suddenly I realized Bill was speaking. My five-second reflection on his life came to a halt. Drifting back into the reality of the hospital setting and my comment that life would be great without stress, I heard Bill respond, "You show me a person who is stressless, and I'll show you a flower that will never bloom." His words lodged in my memory forever.

Here was a man who had known poverty, war, uprootedness, and grief telling me that stress is the stuff that makes flowers bloom. Bill peered at me with a wry grin on his face, and I could not deny that a seed planted fifty-five years before in the sandy soil of an impoverished mill village had certainly grown and flowered. It was the experiences of his lifetime—the stresses he had encountered—that had caused him to bloom and flower.

One of the most popular misconceptions of our age is that a major goal of life should be to reduce stress to a bare minimum. Stress, however, is like fertilizer. Whether flowers or vegetables, plants will not grow without adequate fertilization. Certainly they will not reach their fullest potential of producing beautiful flowers or ripe fruit. On the other hand, too much fertilizer will burn and even kill them. Our goal, then, should be to find a healthy balance—living with enough stress and challenge to stimulate growth, but guarding against taking on so much pressure that we shrivel up and burn out.

Each of us is as unique and individual as any of the assorted flowers in a greenhouse or nursery. Certain species of flowers need more fertilizer than others. The quantity of fertilizer required to make a rosebush reach its greatest beauty might kill a petunia or daffodil. Just so, we each have our own internal balance or quota for stress beyond which the scales tip so that what had been healthy stress, promoting growth, becomes negative stress, leading to burnout, depression, and disease. It takes years of living and self-knowledge to recognize our own balance point.

As I write these lines, I know that within the last few weeks I have reached my balance point of stress and am dangerously close to losing equilibrium in my life. In the last two months I have accepted a new pastorate, sold a house, moved my family to a new city, enrolled my oldest son in first grade, begun relationships with an entirely new set of co-workers, friends, and parishioners, signed a book contract with a pressing deadline—and, in the process, become physically exhausted. And I have learned from past experience that it is now time to back off and restore a healthy balance.

For the next few months I have decided to accept no new engagements or commitments. I am staying on a steady regimen of exercise. I am working diligently with my calendar to reserve some time for rest and relaxation with my family. And, finally, I am spending some time daily ''restoring my soul'' in the green pastures and beside the still waters of Bible study. The events of life have forced me to devise a plan that will allow me to enjoy the zest of new challenge without overdoing it or transforming challenge into destruction.

In his work *Protagoras* (343B), Plato states that the words ''Know Thyself'' were inscribed on the temple at Delphi as one of the world's fundamental pieces of wisdom. This ancient axiom still holds true. Unless we know ourselves, we are not truly wise. And part of this self-knowledge is to be able to assess and define one's balance point of stress.

Too much of a good thing is bad for anybody. Stress is both healthy food and deadly poison. A delicate balance, along with conscientious monitoring of stress, is what we require if we want to live life to its fullest. Let us always affirm with Bill Hale that a person who is stressless is a flower that will never bloom.

REFLECTIONS

It is good for me that I have been afflicted; that I might learn thy statutes.

Psalm 119:71, KJV

We are afflicted in every way, but not crushed;
perplexed, but not despairing;
persecuted, but not forsaken;
struck down, but not destroyed.

2 Corinthians 4:8–9

[Jesus] fell on His face and prayed, saying, "My Father, if it is possible, let this cup pass from Me; yet not as I will, but as Thou wilt."

Matthew 26:39

"In the world you have tribulation, but take courage; I have overcome the world."

John 16:33

[Jesus said] "Come to Me, all who are weary and heavy-laden, and I will give you rest."

Matthew 11:28

There is no spiritual life without persistent struggle and interior conflict.

Thomas Merton[1]

A heavy load brings the ship low in the water but it also keeps her steady.

Alfred Delp[2]

DEAR FATHER:

As I talk with You now, there is a tightness around my forehead and a queasiness within my stomach that have come from a day—indeed weeks—of continuous stress. My work demands are impossible. My self-expectations are too high. And my family, O Father, my family is being neglected! There are not enough hours in the day, not enough years in a lifetime, to do all that I want to do.

O God, I can't avoid this tension and this struggle. Nor do I wish to. But I don't need this headache, either. Please give me the ability to know when to charge and when to retreat; when to hold firm and when to let go; when to stiffen my lip and when to weep. Help me not to fear stress, O Lord. But also help me never to lose a healthy respect for the damage that uncontrolled stress can do to my life and to those I love.

Father, allow me to be a flower that blooms. Root me in Your word and water me with Your presence, so that I may grow and blossom to reflect Your image in this world. I pray this prayer in the name of Him who overcame the world, Jesus Christ, my Lord.

AMEN

3

NO TRIALS SHALL
OVERCOME YOU . . .

As I reflect on the years of my childhood, most of my memories are very pleasant. I was blessed with a stable and happy home, robust health, and an energetic enthusiasm for life. However, as I look back on this era of bright blue skies, there is one dreadfully dark cloud that all but blots out the year 1965. It was the worst period in my family's life.

The year began normally and pleasantly. We were living in the Philippine Islands and I had just turned a gangly fourteen. On New Year's Day, I left home to go on an overnight fishing trip with a friend and his father. When we returned, I saw my mother standing on our porch with a letter in her hand. As I unloaded my gear from the trunk of the car, waved goodbye to my friends, and walked up the porch steps, I knew that something was wrong.

Mom smiled at me weakly, gave me a hug, and asked me to sit down on the steps. She unfolded the crinkled letter. It was from her mother's doctor. He had written to inform us that my grandmother had been diagnosed as having cancer. She had only a few months to live.

Mother began to talk as I awkwardly fumbled around for comforting words I couldn't find. She very calmly informed me that since she was the only daughter, she must return immediately to the United States to care for her mother. My sister and I would have to accompany her. My father, who was president of the Philippine Baptist Seminary, would re-

main until the academic year was over in six months. The
new year had begun with a fury!

Within two weeks we were saying goodbye to my father
and winging out over the vast azure expanse of the Pacific
Ocean. I was excited about returning to America—the Dis-
neyland of the world. But I was also in pain over leaving my
first girlfriend and angry about missing the high school soccer
season. Stunned by the rapid change of events in my life, I
brooded and watched the clouds slip by.

Grandmother was feeling surprisingly well when we arrived at her home in Fort Valley, Georgia. The cancer had
not yet wreaked its full havoc upon her body. Although weak
from radiation treatments, she still worked as a radio dis-
patcher at the police station and after work went fishing
almost every afternoon. Holding a cane pole beside her as the
winter sun descended to the western horizon, and watching
the cork bob, I began to know my grandmother for the first
time. Before, we had always been separated by distance.
Now, in the waning months of her life, I came to know one
who had bequeathed to me history and heritage, as well as the
genetics of life itself. Many days turned to darkness as we sat
by the creek bed and talked.

We had been in Fort Valley five weeks when at three
o'clock one morning I was startled awake by the abrasive
ringing of the telephone in the hallway. I heard Mother's
slippered feet padding down the hall and then her frantic
voice crying, "Oh, no! Oh, no! Not Al!" I knew at once that
my father must be dead. With my heart in my throat, I rushed
to stand numbly beside her while she sobbed and strained to
hear a static-filled voice a world away.

After what seemed an eternity, she hung up the phone.
With relief, I learned that Dad was not dead. But, at the
young age of forty-six, he had suffered a massive heart attack
and was in critical condition. Frantically fumbling through
the pages of the phone book, Mom made reservations for us
to fly back to the Philippines the very next day. Traveling
halfway around the world every other month was beginning
to become a common experience.

When we arrived in the Philippines forty-eight hours later,

Dad's condition was improving. When I entered his hospital room, I felt differently about him than I ever had before. I had always taken for granted that he would be a part of my life. But now looking at him, weakened and pale, for the first time I felt the tentativeness of life. I soberly realized that my parents would not be with me forever.

After several months of recuperation, my father received medical clearance to return to the United States. So hastily packing and storing our household possessions, we crossed the Pacific for the third time in six months. Moving in with my now severely ill grandmother, we transformed a house into an infirmary. A family that had never before known sickness was now surrounded by frailty.

August rolled around and the first days of a new school year drew near. My father's doctor recommended that our family go on vacation. After hiring a nurse to stay with my grandmother, we packed the car and started on a journey to Colorado for a visit with my father's relatives. As we departed from Fort Valley, a feeling of normalcy began to return. We had left the sickbed atmosphere of my grandmother's home. Our family was all together again. A sense of health and lightheartedness began to cheer us all as we looked forward to the clean and vibrant air of the Rocky Mountains.

Around noon, we decided to stop in a small roadside restaurant. After we had ordered, my father stood up and said that he had left his medicine in the car. When the food was served and he had not returned, I grew concerned and went to look for him. I found him stretched across the back seat of the car, gasping for breath. He was having another heart attack.

We rushed him to a small medical clinic in the town—there was no hospital. Within two hours he was dead. Some members of the local Baptist church were called, and I dimly remember that they took us to a motel, where we waited for the funeral director from Fort Valley to come and pick up my father's body and drive us home. The breath of fresh air we sought had turned into a gasp of death. As we huddled in that motel room, it seemed that everything about life was dead or dying. We clung to each other for warmth and comfort.

In November my grandmother's suffering ended. As we again returned from the family plot in the cemetery, we all felt guilty that we were relieved. We were relieved because her pain was over. But we were also relieved that perhaps, now, death would leave us alone—now we could return to the land of the living.

The Christmas of 1965 was understandably grim. I retain only a fleeting picture of attempting to nail a crooked Christmas tree to a wooden stand—my father's job—and in frustration throwing tree and stand angrily out the front door. Furiously I stormed out and bought an artificial tree, a symbol of my yuletide cheer. Yet we made it through Christmas and eagerly awaited the new year. A new start—and the end of an ill-fated year.

Although that Christmas is a hazy blur, what I do vividly remember was a moment on New Year's Eve as midnight approached. My mother, sister, and I were sitting in the den watching television, as a festive crowd in New York City gathered in Times Square to usher in the New Year. As horns began to blow and fireworks explode, the crowd broke into embracing cheers. Mother quietly reached over and turned off the television. The black-and-white picture faded away and suddenly we were a long way from New York—a long way from anywhere. There was a hushed stillness, an emerging intimacy almost too intense to bear.

Mom began to speak softly. She reflected on our difficult journey through 1965. As tears slowly rolled down her cheeks and my eleven-year-old sister snuggled next to her, my eyes darted down to the floor to stare at my frayed tennis shoes. Not knowing whether I could mask my own surging grief, I began to withdraw emotionally. But Mom's penetrating words arrested my flight. I don't remember now all that she said. But as the first minutes of 1966 ticked by, she began to quote from memory Paul's words of encouragement to the church in Corinth:

> *No temptation has overtaken you but such as is common to man; and God is faithful, who will not allow you to be tempted beyond what you are able, but with the temptation*

will provide the way of escape also, that you may be able to endure it (1 Corinthians 10:13).

Even in the midst of my immaturity, I realized that this verse was a foundational pillar in my mother's life. By the tone of her voice, I knew that she had repeated Paul's phrases many times and in many trying situations. And at that moment her spoken words became living words in the life of her floundering son.

Over the years I, too, have repeatedly grasped this verse—this life-rail—when I have been beset by storms. I have come to see that in this one sentence three thoughts of great importance are expressed.

First, Paul tells us that *"no temptation has overtaken you but such as is common to man."* It is important to note that the Greek noun *peirasmos*, translated here as "temptation," can also be translated "trial" or "test." Thus, this verse applies as easily to facing trials in life as it does to overcoming the temptations of sin.

As the colloquial expression states, it is often true that "misery loves company." But I don't believe this is what Paul had in mind. Rather, Paul is saying that when we are confronted by an extremely trying problem or set of circumstances, we must remember that countless other Christians have also faced the same or similar situations and have successfully dealt with equal levels of stress. True, in my particular circumstances, it might have been difficult to find another family who had crossed the Pacific three times, lost a father and a grandmother, and adjusted to a new home all in the span of a year. However, thousands have lost loved ones and homes and have become refugees in the split second it takes for a bomb to explode. Each year hundreds of thousands of American children lose parents to death or divorce and are uprooted. The specifics and details of individual stories may be different, but the general themes are "common to man."

When we are confronted by what seems to be insurmountable troubles, we must remember that other Christians have made the journey before us, and still others journey alongside us. There is comfort within the community of the struggling.

A tremendous amount of assurance has also frequently come to me when I remember the second segment of Paul's statement: *"God is faithful, who will not allow you to be tempted [tested] beyond what you are able."* There are times in all of our lives when our nerves are so stretched and strained that we fear we cannot cope with any more stress. "If one more thing happens," we cry, "something is going to snap!" We wonder when the straw will be dropped that breaks the proverbial camel's back.

The good news is that if we put our trust in God and claim His promise, then we will never face a situation that will destroy us. Now this does not mean that we might not need to seek help through wise counsel and the support of friends. It does not mean that the faithful Christian is immune to physical and emotional exhaustion that might require medical attention. But it does mean that if we "keep the faith," ultimately we will overcome. God will not allow us to be confronted with a situation against which, with His help, we cannot prevail.

Finally, Paul states that with our trials God *"will provide the way of escape also, that you may be able to endure it."* Quite simply, God is not going to sit idly by while His children are engaged in mortal battle and not provide the ammunition and supplies for them to win the war. Granted, help is often before our very noses and, because of pride or stubbornness, we refuse to accept it. But if we look through the eyes of faith and humility, we will see that God always provides a way for us to receive adequate help—spiritual, physical, and emotional—to endure our trials.

Years ago a fourteen-year-old boy came face-to-face with the greatest trial of his life. Through the timely words of a loving mother, God gave him a scriptural promise that provided a "way of escape" so that he might endure it. Praise God for His faithfulness!

⫸⫷ REFLECTIONS ⫸⫷

Cast your burden upon the Lord,
and He will sustain you;
He will never allow the righteous to be shaken.

Psalm 55:22

I will lift up my eyes to the mountains;
From whence shall my help come?
My help comes from the Lord,
Who made heaven and earth.
He will not allow your foot to slip;
He who keeps you will not slumber.
Behold, He who keeps Israel
Will neither slumber nor sleep.

The Lord is your keeper;
The Lord is your shade on your right hand.
The sun will not smite you by day,
Nor the moon by night.
The Lord will protect you from all evil;
He will keep your soul.
The Lord will guard your going out and your coming in
From this time forth and forever.

Psalm 121

"And do not lead us into temptation, but deliver us from evil."

Matthew 6:13

But the Lord is faithful, and He will strengthen and protect
you from the evil one.

2 Thessalonians 3:3

Christ changed the lives of countless warped personalities by the contagious assurance, illustrated in his own character, of the reality of God's protection.

Elton Trueblood[1]

The reason most of us don't ever feel the everlasting arms is because we never lean back.

Dotson Nelson[2]

DEAR FATHER:

As I walk amidst many people today, people who smile and say that "everything's fine," help me to remember that beneath the polite veneer, we all struggle together. Help me to see that my pain is their pain and their pain mine. Enable me to feel a sense of kinship with them.

But, O God, help me to be more than sensitive and empathetic. Grant that I may be the bearer of good news—a good news illustrated in my own life—that You, O Lord, are with us in all events of life and that You will not allow us to be overcome by trials or testing.

Fill my life with confidence, O Father. Instill within me a sense of courage. May I be the lips of love that softly says to a world seeking a new year, a new age, a new Lord:

> No temptation has overtaken you but such as is common to man; and God is faithful, who will not allow you to be tempted beyond what you are able, but with the temptation will provide the way of escape also, that you may be able to endure it.

I pray this in the name of a simple carpenter who exuded the Spirit of God, Jesus Christ, my Lord.

AMEN

WAVES OF FEAR
AND ANXIETY

4

A LIGHT IN THE DARKNESS

Shortly after my graduation from seminary, Beth and I moved to Athens, Georgia, where I was the associate pastor at First Baptist Church. Mortgaging our life away, we bought a small house outside the city limits in a new subdivision that was being built in a dense, secluded, wooded area. Living in one of the first houses built there, we felt as if we were totally alone when the sun set and everything was dark and still. There were no street lights, no traffic, and no next-door neighbors.

The first few nights we spent in our new home, I tentatively dozed with one eye warily open. After living in the close confines of married housing at the seminary, I felt strangely alone and somehow exposed to danger. The deep woods that came to within ten yards of our back door seemed menacing. And to make matters worse, someone had broken into the house two weeks before we moved in and had vandalized one of the rooms. The large windowpane they had shattered to enter still had not been repaired.

One particular night, Beth and I came home late in a furious rainstorm. As we shut and locked all the windows, I once again made a vow that I would replace the broken windowpane before the next sunset. We went to bed with rain hammering on the roof and thunder crashing in the distance, and quickly fell asleep.

Around midnight, a particularly loud clap of thunder reverberated through the woods. I awoke with an adrenaline alarm going off inside me. Something was terribly wrong. Peering through the darkness around the room, I suddenly gasped and froze. Standing in the doorway of our bedroom was the shadowy figure of a huge man silently staring down at our bed. Without my contact lenses I could not see clearly, but I could see well enough to know that the man was at least six feet tall, and that his shoulders were very broad. Being the brave person I am, I quickly decided that the best thing to do was to do nothing at all. So, like a possum, I remained in bed, totally paralyzed with fear and praying that my shaking body would not give me away.

I lay there for what seemed like hours but was really only seconds before Beth began to roll over. I was afraid that she would wake up and scream, so I whispered frantically, "Beth, there's a man standing in the bedroom door." Sleepily comprehending what I said, her body grew rigid with fright. Lightning flashed again, another thunderclap sounded overhead. Suddenly her arm shot out and, like an idiot, I thought, she flicked on the lamp beside the bed. There in the doorway hung my damp raincoat on a coat hanger suspended from the top of the doorframe. I had forgotten that I had placed it there to dry. Too relieved to feel sheepish, I began to laugh hysterically. I had been almost literally scared to death by a limp raincoat!

I have related this story to illustrate a very basic point about fear and anxiety. The emotion of fear is both good and bad. Fear is good when it prepares us to meet and overcome real dangers. Had that dripping raincoat come one step closer, I would have been prepared to at least throw a bedroom slipper at it. However, fear is bad when it sets our adrenaline flowing and activates our anxiety responses over projected dangers that, in reality, never materialize. So much of our life's energy is spent fleeing, fighting, and hiding from harmless wet raincoats hanging in the darkness of our future.

What can we do to defuse some of our high-voltage fears? How can we constructively exorcise the demon of anxiety from within us? I believe the story I have related suggests two simple yet essential principles.

The first step toward alleviating fear is to see clearly what frightens us! In other words, we must be willing to shine a light into the darkness of our fears and discover what lies there—whether a dangerous intruder or a limp raincoat.

I have repeatedly observed in visiting hospital patients who are undergoing diagnostic tests for possible cancer that their most anxious moments come in the intervening hours between the completion of the tests and the reporting of the laboratory results. During this time of uncertainty, even the most stable person is unnerved. However, when the test results return, when the light is turned upon the subject, fear begins to subside, even when cancer is found. In general, people deal with their fears courageously and with repose when they know what they are facing. What is difficult to bear is the fear of the unknown.

It has always interested me that practically every time Jesus cast out a demon from an individual, he gave the demon a name. (See for instance Mark 5:9; 9:25). He identified the destructive force and described it. This was his way of shining a light on the unhealthy agent within a person's body, mind, or spirit. Having identified the dangerous presence, Jesus could then exorcise the demon.

And yet, the reality is that many of us go through life paralyzed by the fear of things we refuse to look at or identify. Like children who are afraid of the darkness, we as adults are irrationally afraid of the light.

I once knew a very fine minister who spoke with eloquence and had a commanding stage presence. No one ever suspected that within him raged a fear that manifested itself in a paralyzing fantasy. His fear was that one Sunday morning he would stand before the congregation and do something totally embarrassing—curse, forget his sermon, run out of the church, or some other illogical action. His fright reached such dimensions that he intensely dreaded worship services. In fact, he considered leaving the ministry.

Finally, he had to decide whether to allow the source of his fear to remain hidden or to seek help in unraveling the mystery of his feelings. Deciding to shine a light on the darkness of his fears, he consulted a counselor.

After several weeks of consultation, the minister discovered that his paralyzing fantasy only symbolized a deeper psychological issue within him. This "man of God" was keenly aware that he was very human. He recognized his own propensity for lust, covetousness, deceit, and selfish desires. Yet because he was a minister, he felt that he could not be himself. He had to be a model of virtue. He feared that if anybody really knew him, they would not like him and he would be rejected. The neurotic fantasy that plagued him as he entered the pulpit only symbolized the deeper issue of being publicly exposed or embarrassed. When the light was focused on the real dynamic he was facing, however, the fearful fantasy dissipated. He once again became relaxed in the pulpit. And more important, he learned that he did not need to be perfect and grew more comfortable with himself.

The self-knowledge this pastor learned through therapy, however, did not come free of charge. First he had to muster the courage to face his fear. Next, he had to find the maturity to enable him to seek a counselor and endure the awkwardness, the embarrassment, and the "emotional nakedness" of sharing with another his deepest fears and intimate fantasies. Finally, he did not gain insight overnight. Rather, it required a commitment of going to therapy for one hour a week over the course of a year for him to gain understanding and for the fear to dissipate. The price was high—but well worth it!

To remove fear from our lives, we must identify its source. After we have been able to give the demon a name, we can, with God's help, cast it out.

I have already alluded to the second step toward removing fear. Often when we are lying in our bed of fear, playing possum, it requires another person to turn on the light. In other words, when we find the courage to confess our fears to our spouse, a trusted friend, a pastor, or a counselor, only then can they help us see through the darkness of our inner psyche.

One of my problems on the night I trembled and stared at the ominous figure in the doorway was that I could not see clearly. I am very nearsighted and had removed my contact lenses. My wife, however, has healthy vision. She could see the object of my fears with a clarity and objectivity I did not have. When lightning flashed and briefly illuminated the object of fear, she saw it for what it truly was—a raincoat. Then she turned on the electric light so I could also see it.

I am convinced that our deepest and most incapacitating fears cannot be relieved and defused until we are able to confess our feelings and anxieties to someone whom we trust. The gifted doctor and psychotherapist Paul Tournier states this in his book *The Meaning of Persons:* "We can become fully conscious only of what we are able to express to someone else."[1] In other words, we will remain nearsighted and have distorted vision until we can squeak out the words to a soulmate, "There's a man standing in the doorway!" Only then can someone who cares for us reach out a helping hand to shine a light on the raincoats in our lives.

One of the true tragedies of life is to see people of great potential literally die of fright in the presence of perceived dangers that in reality do not exist. Our Lord longs to help each of us exorcise these demons of fear from our lives. He wants us to be healthy and whole. Yet He needs our cooperation. We must allow ourselves to be healed by exposing our darkest fears to the light of day.

‖‹› REFLECTIONS ‹∃‖

The Lord is my light and my salvation;
Whom shall I fear?
The Lord is the defense of my life;
Whom shall I dread?
When evildoers came upon me to devour my flesh,
My adversaries and my enemies, they stumbled and fell.
Though a host encamp against me,
My heart will not fear;
Though war arise against me,
In spite of this I shall be confident.

Psalm 27:1–3

"Peace I leave with you; My peace I give to you; not as the world gives, do I give to you. Let not your heart be troubled, nor let it be fearful."

John 14:27

For God has not given us a spirit of timidity, but of power and love and discipline.

2 Timothy 1:7

Not everything that is faced can be changed; but nothing can be changed until it is faced.

James Baldwin[2]

Courage is doing what you are afraid to do. There can be no courage unless you're scared.

Eddie Rickenbacker[3]

You gain strength, courage and confidence by every experience in which you really stop to look fear in the face.

Eleanor Roosevelt[4]

The tragedy of life is what dies within a man while he still lives.

Albert Schweitzer[5]

DEAR FATHER:

You alone know the fear and panic that sometimes breaks loose within me. I often feel that if people could read my thoughts, they would think that I am silly, neurotic, and so very sinful. I know that my potential is being limited and jeopardized by my fear of failure, my fear of exposure, and, yes—as strange as it may sound—my fear of success.

O Lord, grant me the courage to grope until I find a mirror on the wall in my inner room of darkness and to look at myself honestly. Then give me the grace of the presence of a loving person to help me turn on the light. May I have the courage to look at my own face and stare into my own eyes. And may I truly discover, O Father, that I am Your son, Your daughter, made in Your own image.

Help me give a name to my fears. And cast these demons from me, I pray.

AMEN

5

A BECKONING DISTANCE

I couldn't believe I was actually going to do it! Scrubbed down, suited up, with mask in place, I squeamishly accompanied Beth into the delivery room to witness the birth of our first child. Until that moment, all that I knew of the birth process had come a year before when I heard a mewing in our bedroom closet. I opened the door to find that our "male" cat, Percy, was delivering kittens in a shoe box. Now here I was amidst bright lights, stainless steel instruments, bustling nurses, standing beside a wife who was depending on me to guide her through the complex breathing patterns of a French birthing method with a name I could barely pronounce. I sighed, gulped, and promised myself that I would not faint!

Three years later, I have finally quit gushing over the wonders of the birth experience to anyone who will listen. I have also pasted the out-of-focus photographs of the event into an album to sit quietly on a shelf until our son Drew is old enough to appreciate them. However, as I reflect on that experience, three things are imprinted on my memory that have come to symbolize for me some of the greatest truths of life.

First, I hold the symbolic picture of Drew's anguished face and the bellowing cry he emitted when the doctor eased him forth and then held him up for me to see. I have never viewed a little face so contorted with the mixed emotions of anger and terror. There was an unmistakable cry of rage that came from being forcibly squeezed from the intimate symbiotic existence of the womb. But there was also the heartrending cry of fear. A cry that spoke of the terror of separation, the trauma of having one's umbilical cord severed and being cast adrift to function as a single, solitary unit of life. My son came into this world "telling it like it is"!

The second symbolic image I recall was formed when the doctor laid that quivering little bundle on Beth's chest and she placed his face against her breast. Prompted by the miracle of instinct, he immediately began to suckle. Tears sprang to my eyes and silently rolled down my cheeks. Drew's crying ceased. The fright was momentarily quelled. Flesh touched flesh, and the warmth of human milk bonded mother to child. A relationship that overcomes separation was begun.

As I looked at my son's face, I suddenly noticed his eyes. I gasped! Those were not Drew's eyes! They were my mother's eyes! The way they crinkled in the corners, the shape of the brows. His eyes were definitely from the Mathews clan. And in this observation of wonder I saw the third picture-symbol of the day—the fact that we are all related. We have the same eyes, the same feelings, and we bear the mark of the same Creator.

In the drama of human birth we can see the struggles of a lifetime symbolically portrayed. For the greatest source of anxiety with which we all must cope from birth to the grave is the realization that we are, to varying degrees, separated from the Source of our being—God—from each other, and even from ourselves. Nowhere is this picture painted more graphically than in the first three chapters of Genesis. In this epic writing we find the man and the woman driving a wedge between themselves and God, putting on clothes to hide from each other, and finally being driven out of the garden, the very ground of their being. The message of Genesis—indeed, of the entire Bible—is one of separation seeking reunification. This *is* the course and dynamic of all human events, all human relationships, all human history.

When we step outside of biblical history and theology, we also find modern-day psychologists—Christian and non-

Christian—in virtual agreement that the deepest driving need of men and women is to overcome a sense of separation and alienation. Psychiatrist Erich Fromm writes in his classic work, *The Art of Loving:*

> The desire for interpersonal fusion is the most powerful striving in man. . . . Man—of all ages and cultures—is confronted with the solution of one and the same question: the question of how to overcome separation, how to achieve union, how to transcend one's own individual life and find at-onement.[1]

After defining this basic hunger in men and women, Fromm goes on to illuminate the consequence of not finding a sense of relatedness and union in this world:

> The experience of separateness arouses anxiety; it is, indeed, the source of all anxiety. . . . The deepest need of man, then, is the need to overcome his separateness, to leave the prison of aloneness. The absolute failure to achieve this means insanity.[2]

Thus, an innate sense of separation is the root cause of all anxiety and fear. And mental illness can be called the disease of separation.

On a less intellectual and theoretical level, a book popular while I was in college says the same thing—Jess Lair's *I Ain't Much, Baby—But I'm All I've Got.* With a title like that, I and thousands of others were lured into reading its pages. But what made it a bestseller was not its catchy title but its theme, best expressed by Lair with these words:

> Now the basic principle that I see here is our tremendous need for other people. We need them, as I see, desperately. And this I do not question at all. If there is any universal cry that I hear from people, young and old, it is their aloneness, their separateness from other people. And . . . for you and for me, the knowledge that we are not alone is the most crucial knowledge that can be brought to any of us.[3]

Lair's message obviously rang true for his readers. We all fear loneliness. And even though we may be surrounded by crowds, have many acquaintances, love our spouse, and worship with a throng of hundreds on Sunday morning, we know that a sense of separation is in our heart. We yearn in our souls to be in close union with others, with nature, with the creative rhythm of life.

I once heard the talented preacher John Claypool relate a story that I shall never forget. It seems that when the carnage of World War I had bled its last, the government of France was faced with an unusual problem. In their army hospitals were over one hundred soldiers who had developed total amnesia caused by battle trauma. These men could not remember their names, their families, their hometowns. They were totally separated from their origins.

Finally, the government announced to the whole nation that all families who had relatives missing in action should come to a certain hospital on an appointed day. For this occasion, a large platform was erected. With the families gathered around the platform, the soldiers were led out one by one in the hope that somebody would recognize them and they could be reunited with their loved ones.

What a tragic scene! Yet at times each of us has stood on that platform saying, "Who is my family? Who are my friends? Who am I? And when will I ever be at home again?" We are war veterans, all of us. We long to have our memory restored to when we lived in Eden.

What can we do about all this? How can we narrow the gap of separation and feel more a sense of unity and belonging in our hearts? I firmly believe that we can lessen our fear of separation by making the *maintenance of personal relationships* the highest priority in our lives. We can approach this goal in three ways:

First, we must take the time to maintain and consistently care for relationships with our family and friends. This truth was brought home to me while I was reading the recent research findings of the Grant Study, a long-term research project undertaken by Harvard University. The purpose of the study was to follow over a thirty-year period the lives and careers of 268 male students selected from the graduating classes of 1939 through 1944. It was hoped that personality traits and behavioral characteristics discerned in these men could be used as determining factors for anticipating the mental and emotional health of future students. In other words, the researchers wanted to find out what factors lead to health and what traits lead to instability.

True to expectations, over the thirty-year period, some of the men led lives characterized by emotional stability and contributed much to society. Others developed unhealthy habits, became emotionally brittle, and generally floundered. Why did some of the men succeed while others failed?

A dominant finding of the Grant Study was that neither the presence nor the absence of traumatic and difficult events in these men's lives served as determinants of emotional health. Some who encountered the greatest trials remained the most stable, while others who experienced apparently smooth sailing, capsized. Rather, the study found—and this is significant—that those men who had enduring and sustaining relationships in their lives reflected the highest level of emotional health.[4]

I am convinced that the most constructive way to cope with our innate fear of separation is to do our absolute best to care for, maintain, and sustain the primary relationships in our lives. It is these relationships—parents, brothers and sisters, spouses, children, close friends—that will determine whether our cup of life is full or empty.

Several years ago I heard Dr. Daniel Levinson of Yale University speak at a seminar. Recognized nationally as one of the leading authorities in the area of adult development, Levinson spoke with a wealth of academic insight and knowledge. However, the statement which had the greatest impact on me was simple, nontechnical, yet profound:

> Life has meaning when relationships have meaning. . . . The richness of my life at any one time may be determined by how many and what quality of relationships I might have at that one time.[5]

Thus Levinson echoes the Grant Study in saying that it is the quality of interpersonal relationships that makes all the difference in our lives. It is the warmth of these abiding relationships that melts the cold of separation and brings to us a sense of unity.

However, do not forget that I used the word *maintenance*—the maintenance of relationships. Quality relationships do not just happen. They are developed and cherished at a great price—time, care, initiative, nurture, and the mutual sharing of events in life. We must apply loving and continuing maintenance to our relationships if they are to be of a quality that builds bridges over the chasm of separation.

The second way we can lessen our fear of separation is to maintain and care for not only our relationships with men and women but also our relationship with God. Unless the God who created us is allowed to live intimately with us, we will not be in harmony with ourselves, our families, our friends, or the world of nature about us. The tragedy that transpired in Eden was that when Adam and Eve sinned, they lost their face-to-face relationship with God. Our hearts still hunger for that eye-to-eye contact with our Father.

Unfortunately, we will never look into the eyes of God upon this earth. That is the cost of sin. But through prayer, meditation, Bible study, and the mediation of the Holy Spirit, we can sense the presence of God in our lives and relate to Him. Although we cannot touch His hands, we can feel their presence on our shoulders. We must intentionally try to maintain our relationship with God or we will remove our shoulders from His hands.

Finally, we must accept the fact that there will always be some semblance of a hollow void in our lives that makes us feel lonely. Rather than fearing this emptiness, we must come to accept it as a gracious gift from God. For it is the pain of separation that causes us to continue to yearn for the presence of God and to seek greater intimacy with our brothers and sisters. Thank God that the quest for unity is a hunger that cannot be quelled, a thirst that cannot be quenched upon this earth.

Thus, unlike an abscessed tooth, which can be pulled and thrown away, the pain of separation will always be with us.

We can learn to fear this pain, to cringe when its throbbing presence is felt. Or we can learn to cope with the pain by building some strong and enduring relationships that will support us along life's way. After all, even Jesus needed a few good friends and a God He called "Father" to see Him through the loneliness of life. Should we need anything less?

IIICI REFLECTIONS CIIII

When the woman saw that the tree was good for food, and that it was a delight to the eyes, and that the tree was desirable to make one wise, she took from its fruit and ate; and she gave also to her husband with her, and he ate. Then the eyes of both of them were opened, and they knew that they were naked; and they sewed fig leaves together and made themselves loin coverings. And they heard the sound of the Lord God walking in the garden in the cool of the day, and the man and his wife hid themselves from the presence of the Lord God among the trees of the garden.

Genesis 3:6–8

Where can I go from Thy Spirit?
Or where can I flee from Thy presence?
If I ascend to heaven, Thou art there;
If I make my bed in Sheol, behold, Thou art there.
If I take the wings of the dawn,
If I dwell in the remotest part of the sea,
Even there Thy hand will lead me,
And Thy right hand will lay hold of me.
If I say, "Surely the darkness will overwhelm me,
And the light around me will be night,"
Even the darkness is not dark to Thee,
And the night is as bright as the day.
Darkness and light are alike to Thee.

Psalm 139:7–12

For I am convinced that neither death, nor life, nor angels, nor principalities, nor things present, nor things to come, nor powers, nor height, nor depth, nor any other created thing, shall be able to separate us from the love of God, which is in Christ Jesus our Lord.

Romans 8:38–39

The whole conviction of my life now rests upon the belief that loneliness, far from being a rare and curious phenomenon, peculiar to myself and to a few other solitary men, is the central and inevitable fact of human existence.

Thomas Wolfe[6]

For a crowd is not company; and faces are but a gallery of pictures; and talk but a tinkling cymbal, where there is not love.

Francis Bacon[7]

No man is an island, entire of itself; every man is a piece of the continent, a part of the main. . . .

John Donne[8]

The nearness of God . . . is primarily dependent on man, not on God.

Emil Brunner[9]

Thou hast made us for Thyself, and restless are our hearts until they find rest in Thee.

St. Augustine[10]

DEAR GOD:

I have tried to write this prayer at least a dozen times. Weeks have gone by between attempts. Yet, with each fresh start I have put my pencil down to await a clearer mind or a more inspired moment. And still, words fail me.

How can I speak of the loneliness within me, O Lord? I, who have been blessed with a loving wife, affectionate children, quality friendships, and a caring Heavenly Father— how can I speak of loneliness? And yet, it is there, O Lord. A feeling of separation that stifles my tongue and spirit.

It seems that loneliness is the thorn of all flesh. The curse of Eden. Somehow, I always thought it would get better. And, over the years, I guess it has. But the pain still nags and throbs beneath the surface of my smile.

Do you remember when I was a little boy, O Father, and Steve would come over to spend the night? In the darkness we would giggle and tell silly jokes. Fighting sleep together we experienced a closeness of friendship I have never known in manhood. I long for those days of "best friends."

And then there were team sports and clubs. Girls and dating. And finally, the pinnacle, marriage. And yet, even in marriage, the closer Beth and I have become—the more we share ourselves in our children, our dreams, our fears, and our convictions—the more I realize there is a distance between two people that cannot be wholly breached by love, or sexual union, or anything upon this earth. To touch one you really love with your eyes or your thoughts or a gentle kiss is to know a beckoning distance.

O Lord, give me the ability to live amidst loneliness with a thankful heart for all of the beautiful relationships that I have shared but not possessed. Give me the wisdom to know that loneliness is but the suction of the heart that draws us toward God. I pray this in the name of Him who said, ''The foxes have holes, and the birds of the air have nests, but the Son of Man has nowhere to lay His head.''[11]

AMEN

6

A FEAR OF FEAR

In the early 1930s, a contagious fear pervaded America, a fear like the cold vapor emanating from a fog-shrouded lake in winter. The chill penetrated even to the nerveless marrow of one's bones.

There was good reason for the fear. The stock market had crashed. Banks had closed. Livelihoods had been dashed and jobs were difficult to find. Families huddled together with little food in the pantry and no coal for the furnace. Teenagers who had dreamed of college watched as their hopes dimmed. Some men chose to escape their fears by jumping out of skyscraper windows or becoming hoboes. America was in the doldrums, gripped by anxiety.

Sensing the fear that threatened to paralyze the spirit and fervor of the American people, President Franklin D. Roosevelt began his now-famous radio broadcasts, which he called "fireside chats." In doing so, the President wanted to kindle a flame within his countrymen. He knew that he needed to remove the chill in the air and restore the American public to a spirit of firm resolve and stubborn resistance. His deep, dignified voice began to fill the homes of millions of people with courage.

Roosevelt began to address head-on the heart of the problem of American morale in his first inaugural address. He wanted to clearly define the issue. With simple words that have since become almost a cliché, President Roosevelt intoned, "The only thing we have to fear is fear itself." Most Americans who reflected on his words through the years of his presidency and heard his bolstering voice on the radio looked within themselves and knew he had hit the nail on the head. They were indeed fearing fear.

Now what is meant by the seemingly contradictory phrase, "fear of fear"? Very simply, most of us seek to withdraw or escape from painful or unpleasant experiences. One of the most uncomfortable emotions I have ever felt is the jagged, raw edge of fear. Although we laugh at fear in retrospect when the high ground of safety has been reached, none of us laughs when the lion growls and our stomachs draw up in knots, our heart is squeezed, adrenaline pours hotly through our veins, and we grow dizzy as we tremble. We all avoid the pain of fear.

However, there are those individuals whose experience of fear is so intense that they consciously, or subconsciously, decide that the most important thing in life is to *avoid* the emotion of fear at all costs. In effect, they become afraid of fear itself. Any significant tremor that sets off their fear mechanism sends them into flight.

An example of this type of behavior can be seen in a behavioral science experiment with laboratory animals. Rats are placed in wire cages, which have been connected to electric terminals. When a bell is rung, a mild but uncomfortable electric shock is permitted to flow through the grid of the cage for a few seconds. The rats feel the pain and, in terror, try to escape. At first they do not associate the bell with the shock. Very quickly, however, the association is made and their flight mechanism is fully activated every time they hear the bell, even if it rings and no electricity is released. In essence, the rats have come to fear the bell, even if the electricity is not present.

The clear parallel between the experiment with the rats and human behavior is that some people have been so traumatized by tension and fear that the mere suggestion—the bell—of a fearful or trying situation sends them into panic. Indeed, such reactions in their more extreme form have often been termed "panic attacks" or "anxiety attacks."

Thousands upon thousands of people live with this malady. Most people who suffer from this trauma in its milder form simply learn to avoid fear-inducing situations. For example, they may avoid crowds, refuse to drive, refrain from going on trips that remove them from familiar surroundings, or practice a host of other "avoidance" patterns in an effort to cope with anxiety.

There are others—including, most disturbingly, adolescents— who avoid feeling fear by numbing their nerve impulses. When a situation inducing trauma arises, they resort to alcohol, smoke marijuana, pop Valium, or snort cocaine. Regardless of the type of drug, legal or illegal, the result is the same. Nerves that convey feelings of fear are numbed into nonresponsiveness.

In extreme situations, some people flee from fear by escaping into the hallucinatory realm of mental illness. I served a congregation once in which there was a man who had experienced a very trying and tumultuous life. He had known fear in many forms. Over the years, he had increasingly come to fear his fear. At first, he simply avoided stressful situations. He remained secluded at home. Then he became hooked on an assortment of prescription and nonprescription drugs. Finally, because of emerging schizophrenic tendencies accelerated by his drug dependency, he was hospitalized in a psychiatric hospital.

As he "dried out" and the residue of the drugs left his system, he became more like his old self. Yet he could not bear the thought of leaving the perceived safety of the hospital. Although he feared death, he feared living even more and therefore refused to eat.

As his weight declined and death approached, I went late one afternoon to visit this tormented man. In previous visits I had encouraged him to eat. His family had pleaded with him. But he still refused nourishment. Now, as I entered his room, I decided I would not mention the topic of food.

After a few minutes of very lucid conversation, I asked him, "Joe, what is it going to take to get you well?" He thought for a few moments and then with great intelligence and insight replied, "When I can look God in the eye and myself in the eye and see that I have no fear of fear, then I can get well.'' What a startling, perplexing, tragic, and accurate insight!

Sadly, Joe chose to ''get well'' and escape fear by deliberately dying. His case is clearly an extreme example of what can result from the malady of fearing fear. But it is in examples of extremity that we can most clearly see emotional problems and their causes.

Quite obviously, the greatest tragedy of fearing fear is that it results in our withdrawing from fully experiencing the goodness and joy of life. We are so preoccupied with the bell that we haven't even noticed that the electrical wires from our cages have been disconnected. We constantly cower, ready to flee to the areas we have defined as safe as soon as the first drop of adrenaline courses through our system.

In seeking to overcome this malady—and most of us who have lived long enough can relate to it to varying degrees—I have found wisdom in Geoffrey Moorhouse's book *The Fearful Void*. Moorhouse writes:

> The most insidious form of fear . . . is the fear of being afraid. . . . Yet, if in the face of fear, we can summon the strength and the faith to go forward, I think that far more often than not we find that one of two things happens. Either the encounter with the thing feared demonstrates that it is by no means as laden with terrible properties as we supposed from a distance, a discovery which tends to dissolve the fear itself. Or else, terrible as the encounter may prove to be, it is one which can be endured and which can fortify us in the endurance.[1]

I believe that within Moorhouse's statement are found the two most important avenues for overcoming a fear of fear.

First, Moorhouse states that we can overcome a fear of fear by gritting our teeth and walking into the ghost house of our lives. In other words, we need to experience the very thing that we fear. Once inside our ghost house, we may find that there are no goblins after all, only empty rooms. There was nothing to fear.

Fifteen years after my family left the Philippines and the

previously recounted disaster of 1965 occurred, I had an opportunity to return for the first time and teach a three weeks' course at the seminary where my father had taught. I must confess, I had some real fears about returning. My fantasy was that I would go back "home" and be overcome by a sense of grief and longing for childhood, my father, lost friends, and other tender memories. I conjured up all types of scenarios of breaking down and crying, of being depressed and despondent, and of simply being miserable. In weak moments, I contemplated declining the invitation.

Yet, I knew that I could not live with myself if I did not accept the opportunity. Not to do so would have let my fear of fear gain a tighter grip on my life. I determined that I would return and "stick my nose in it," even if it killed me.

Despite my reservations, some of the greatest joys and healing moments in my life came in those three weeks of reunion. The only tears that were shed were tears of happiness. As I literally walked into the house of my childhood, there were no ghosts. When I preached in the church where I was baptized as an eight-year-old, my heart nearly burst with joyful thanksgiving. And the most healing aspect of the trip—a realization that did not dawn on me until weeks later—was that I was finally emotionally able to "bury" my father. By encountering my fear, I destroyed it. I discovered there was nothing to be afraid of after all. Indeed, I grew healthier and more confident from having engaged in the battle and, with God's strength, won.

It sometimes happens, however, that when we do decide to encounter our fear, we experience true pain, Moorhouse's second point. This is seen in the case of people who actually suffer classic panic attacks. The most effective therapy for such people is to encourage them not to flee from the anxiety when it overcomes them. Rather, they should try to sit still and fully experience the fear. Their fantasy is that the anxiety surge will overwhelm them and that they will go "crazy." But even though they may shake with fright, they most often discover that they are not overwhelmed. And with this discovery—although painful—the hold of anxiety upon their lives can begin to diminish.

As I write these very words, my wife has just shown me an account in a nationwide newspaper about the well-known weatherman, Willard Scott. It seems that he suffers from stage fright. Although he daily brings weather forecasts into millions of homes via the electronic medium of television, he still has a phobic fear of speaking in front of live audiences. When he addresses people instead of television cameras, he is often overcome by a painful sense of anxiety, which causes his heart to beat furiously, his palms to perspire, and his breathing to become very labored. He literally has to fight to overcome panic.

Recently, however, Scott publicly admitted his fear. Addressing the over 1.1 million Americans who are also phobia victims, he states, "Once it happens, you get afraid of fear itself. You use prescription drugs as a crutch, but you have to wean yourself from them to get back control." The best way Scott has found to overcome the fear is to meet it head on. In his own earthy way Scott enjoins, "I say to it, 'You're not going to beat me, you SOB!' "[2] And the truth is, it hasn't.

Whether the source of our fear is real or imagined, if we are afraid of fear, we inevitably retreat from experiencing the fullness of life. We develop a neurotic avoidance behavior that cripples us. The only way we can diminish the fear is to experience the fear. When we have done that, the fear will lift from our life like the cold fog that evaporates from the surface of a lake when the light of the sun shines on it.

ⅢⅢ❏ REFLECTIONS ❏ⅢⅢ

I sought the Lord, and He answered me,
And delivered me from all my fears.

Psalm 34:4

[Jesus] said to them, "It is I; do not be afraid."

John 6:20

I can do all things through Him who strengthens me.

Philippians 4:13

Be anxious for nothing, but in everything by prayer and supplication with thanksgiving let your requests be made known to God.

Philippians 4:6–7

Casting all your anxiety upon Him, because He cares for you.

1 Peter 5:7

There is only one man that I fear, and his name is James Garfield.

James A. Garfield[3]

Let me assert my firm belief that the only thing we have to fear is fear itself—nameless, unreasoning, terror which paralyzes needed efforts to convert retreat into advance.

Franklin D. Roosevelt[4]

'Twas grace that taught my heart to fear,
And grace my fears relieved;

How precious did that grace appear
The hour I first believed.

John Newton[5]

If by temperament we are anxious, we may have to accept our anxiety like a physical disability—and just get on as best we can. There are times when we are paralyzed by fear. And fear can't be got rid of just by our own effort, but only by finding ourselves caught up into a cause greater than our own interests.

Alan Paton[6]

DEAR FATHER:

Grant me the wisdom to know that I cannot escape from fear without paradoxically losing the joy and challenge of my days on earth. Help me not to fear more than I yearn for life.

May the same Grace that taught my heart to fear, now my fears relieve.

I pray this in the name of Him who was terrified and yet endured Gethsemane, Jesus Christ, my Lord.

AMEN

7

ONE STEP AT A TIME

This morning as I was eating breakfast, I gazed out on our deck and saw a beautiful sight. Our two golden retrievers, Beau and Buffy, were stretched out side by side, basking in the warmth of the morning sun. As their rich coats shone and their bodies emanated deep satisfaction, I could not help feeling envious. What I really yearned for was the chance to pull up a deck chair, kick off my shoes, and relax with them. But I had to rush to the office. In my pocket I had a list of a dozen things that had to be done today if my goals for this week were to be accomplished.

When I rushed out of the house and jumped into the car, Beau and Buffy still lay in the sunlight with no cares, no thought whatsoever for tomorrow. Driving to work, I continued to muse on their tranquility when suddenly it hit me that what makes the human being totally different from other animals is an ability to comprehend the future. Tomorrow's anticipated needs were totally dictating the way I lived today. But Beau and Buffy lay in the sun contented because they did not have the capacity to perceive the future, to plan for tomorrow, to worry about next year. Only human beings can project themselves into a realm beyond the present.

Undoubtedly, our ability to anticipate the future is one of the greatest gifts God has given us. Without this ability, we could not prepare for any forthcoming eventuality. Like my dogs, we would all lie in the sun, and society, as we know it, would soon return to the law of the jungle. All action would be predicated on immediate need. Our world would be plunged into chaos.

And yet, our ability to plan for tomorrow is also a two-edged sword. For anxiety, the fear of the future, is one of the greatest stresses in our lives. Most of us find that we navigate the waters of our present day very well. What throws us into a nervous tizzy is worrying about the storms or crises that might loom over the horizon.

I must confess that I am an overly future-oriented person. If I could have a penny for every minute I have spent worrying about my tomorrows, I would easily be a millionaire. Indeed, I suspect most of us would be. Too often we cannot enjoy the sunshine of today because we are worrying about the needs and fears of tomorrow.

In my own attempt to deal with my anxiety about the future, I have trained myself to remember a story I heard as a teenager. One of my closest friends was Guy Pearson. On many evenings when we had run out of things to do, we would find ourselves at his house, lounging around watching television. Usually his father, Mr. James, as we called him, would be sprawled in his easy chair, and we liked to engage him in conversation.

I particularly enjoyed coaxing Mr. James into talking about his experiences as a soldier in the European theater during World War II. One story he told has had a lasting impact on my life.

James Pearson was part of a reconnaissance team sent out to scout German troop positions. The patrol left early on a blustery winter morning. As they departed the security of their own front lines, they had to cross an American minefield. The mines had been clearly marked for their passage and very nimbly they wound their way around the explosives. On the other side of the field, they melted into the woods and tensely approached the unknown of the German positions.

They had not advanced very far when a concealed machine gun emplacement opened up on them, pinning them to the ground. For hours they lay unable to advance or retreat. As time slowly ticked by, the blue sky became slate gray and snow clouds began to roll in. By midafternoon a virtual blizzard had descended on the land and visibility became limited. As the snowfall grew heavier, the platoon's leader decided they had to risk a retreat under cover of the storm. By a saving act of nature, they were able to slip away from the deadly German cross fire and return toward American lines.

But when they reached the edge of the woods and looked out across the pastureland containing the minefield, a new and equally lethal problem confronted them. The deep snow had completely covered all the markings that had indicated where the mines had been planted. As dusk settled upon them, a quick decision had to be made.

The platoon leader sensed that a major German offensive was imminent. If his patrol waited until the next day to cross the minefield, they could be easily wiped out by a German advance at dawn. Although it was risky, they really had only one option. They had to take their chances and cross the minefield before darkness totally enveloped them.

The lieutenant called the men together. He informed them that he was going to lead them single file across the meadow. He sternly ordered them to walk thirty yards behind each other and, most important, to place their boots exactly in the imprints left by his boots. In this way, if a mine exploded, only he would detonate it, and he alone would be killed.

Slowly the reconnaissance team advanced across the meadow. Only one set of bootprints was left by the entire platoon. Miraculously, they all made it safely to American lines. The next day as the men awoke, they found that their bootprints could still be seen in the snow. Several hours later when army engineers again marked the positions of the mines, it was found that the entire platoon had neatly stepped over a mine, narrowly avoiding detonating its deadly explosive power. They had been saved by stepping in one another's bootprints.

This riveting story contains some very simple and yet profound symbolism about how we should face the future. I often reflect on this imagery when I fear the next step in my life.

First of all, going through life is much like crossing a

minefield. There are some very real dangers out there. They are not imaginary. At any moment something might blow up in our face. Yet like the men in the reconnaissance team, we do not have the option of not crossing the meadow. We cannot turn our backs on the future. Life moves forward and we must move with it.

However, as the platoon leader clearly saw, life is crossed one step at a time. We cannot allow ourselves to worry excessively about where we will be placing our feet fifty yards down the line. What is of infinite importance is where our supporting foot is situated now and where our very next step will be placed. All our attention and sensitivity must be riveted on the present moment. If in worrying about the future we become distracted and do not focus on the step immediately before us, we run a greater risk of detonating real trouble. There can be no safe tomorrow if we do not focus on the needs as well as the pleasures of today.

Jesus Christ was a realist. True, he was concerned about the future. While in Galilee, he knew he must go to Jerusalem. Yet he was firmly rooted in the present moment. He taught His disciples about facing the anxieties of the future:

> *"For this reason I say to you, do not be anxious for your life, as to what you shall eat, or what you shall drink; nor for your body, as to what you shall put on. Is not life more than food, and the body than clothing? Look at the birds of the air, that they do not sow, neither do they reap, nor gather into barns, and yet your heavenly Father feeds them. Are you not worth much more than they? And which of you by being anxious can add a single cubit to his life's span? . . . Do not be anxious then, saying, 'What shall we eat?' or 'What shall we drink?' or 'With what shall we clothe ourselves?' For all these things the Gentiles eagerly seek; for your heavenly Father knows that you need all these things. But seek first His kingdom and His righteousness; and all these things shall be added to you. Therefore do not be anxious for tomorrow; for tomorrow will care for itself. Each day has enough trouble of its own"*
> (Matthew 6:25–27, 31–34).

Because He knew that each day has enough to be concerned about without being anxious for tomorrow, Jesus believed in taking life one firm step at a time.

The second important image in this story is the most graphic—the picture of the whole platoon walking in the steps of their leader. This act of obedience alone brought the men across the minefield in safety.

In effect, we, too, must secure our future not by worrying about it but rather by making sure that each present step is following in the footsteps of Jesus. More than anything else, Jesus taught us how to live by His example. It is true that when we live like Him and walk in His pathway, we will be exposed to trials and to danger. Jesus somewhat cryptically said, "Do not think that I came to bring peace on the earth; I did not come to bring peace, but a sword" (Matthew 10:34). He also said, "He who does not take his cross and follow after Me is not worthy of Me" (Matthew 10:38). What our Lord was clearly saying is that to walk in His footsteps—to love as He did, to live in His Spirit, to actualize His teaching—is to be exposed to a battlefield where people really do get hurt, where mines explode, and where people are crucified. To walk in the footsteps of Jesus is to do real battle with the forces of evil in this world.

Yet, having recognized clearly what Dietrich Bonhoeffer called "the cost of discipleship," we must also see that Jesus, like the platoon leader, did not tell His disciples *how* to traverse life and then send them on their solitary way, each man for himself. Rather, He said, "Follow me." The too easily forgotten but unique aspect of the Christian faith is that we have a Lord who walks ahead of us each step of the way. Our task is not to worry about the mines. Rather, our concern should be to place our feet in the footprints of our Leader, one step at a time.

As I conclude this chapter, I am tempted to say, "This is too simplistic! Too cut and dried! This simple imagery will insult the readers' intelligence. Life is more complex than this." And yet, when all is said and done, the most difficult things to accomplish in life are the simple things. And the most important skills to develop are the basic skills. When it comes to living the Christian life and facing the future in confidence, nothing can be more important than living one day at a time, following in the footsteps of Jesus. Such a life alleviates fear. Such a life allows us to sit back and enjoy the sunshine of the present moment. Such a life places a firm life-rail in our hands.

ⅢⒸ REFLECTIONS ⒸⅢ

The Lord is my shepherd; I shall not want.

Psalm 23:1, KJV

Whoso putteth his trust in the Lord shall be safe.

Proverbs 29:25, KJV

"Do not fear, for I am with you;
Do not anxiously look about you, for I am your God.
I will strengthen you, surely I will help you,
Surely I will uphold you with My righteous right
hand."

Isaiah 41:10

"If anyone wishes to come after Me, let him deny him-
self, and take up his cross daily, and follow Me. For
whoever wishes to save his life shall lose it, but whoever
loses his life for My sake, he is the one who will save
it."

Luke 9:23–24

Who is he that will harm you, if ye be followers of that which is good.

1 Peter 3:13, KJV

Children have neither past nor future; they enjoy the present, which very few of us do.

Jean de la Bruyère[1]

The future is purchased by the present.

Samuel Johnson[2]

No man ever sank under the burden of the day. It is when tomorrow's burden is added to the burden of today that the weight is more than a man can bear. Never load yourself so. If you find yourself so loaded, at least remember this: it is your own doing, not God's. He begs you to leave the future to Him, and mind the present.

George MacDonald[3]

Sweetly, Lord, have we heard thee calling, "Come follow me!"
And we see where thy footprints falling, lead us to thee.
Footprints of Jesus that make the pathway glow;
We will follow the steps of Jesus where'er they go.

Mary B.C. Slade[4]

Day by day, dear Lord, of thee three things I pray:
To see thee more clearly

Love thee more dearly
Follow thee more nearly,
Day by day.

Richard of Chichester

DEAR FATHER:

The future beckons and I go. Give me the courage not to blaze a trail of my own but rather to follow You each step of the way. Though I cannot be certain of what lies ahead on my path, I can be sure that You will be with me—guiding me, sustaining me, providing for my every need. You are my shepherd; I shall not want.

AMEN

TIDES OF CHALLENGE AND DECISION

8

SHOW THEM YOU CAN'T PLAY

Making the decision to accept a significant challenge—a challenge that might result in failure—is one of the most difficult aspects of the Christian pilgrimage. And yet, if we are never faced with such venturesome opportunities, we cease to grow emotionally and spiritually. Challenge is an indispensable growth hormone for our personal development.

Recently, I observed a humorous analogy of this truth in the life of our little kitten, Tiger. It was six o'clock in the morning and I was sitting groggily on the side of the bed, fumbling with my running shoes. Suddenly Tiger pounced from hiding in the covers on the front of the bed and landed beside me.

As I tied my shoelaces, I saw Tiger suddenly freeze and lower his ears in an attack posture. His eyes were riveted to an object on top of Beth's dresser, some two feet away. Slowly he crouched and cocked every muscle in his body for one great leap. For a second he perched on the edge of the mattress, caught in doubt and indecision. To reach the dresser top, he would have to bound two feet out from the bed and up to an altitude of three feet above the mattress. Tiger had never before attempted a feat like this.

He hesitated for only a moment. Then his taut legs kicked, and he was propelled into the air. I knew what was going to happen. I had never seen a cat jump face-first into a dresser drawer, but I was about to—pink nose, whiskers, and all.

And yet, it didn't happen. Like a plane hitting the end of a carrier deck, Tiger inched over the edge of the dresser top and landed in a gawky tangle of skinny legs and twisting paws.

But the show had just begun! The day before, Beth had waxed the dresser and it was slick as glass. Suddenly, Tiger was experiencing a second new reality for the day. As he landed in a heap he didn't stop. Instead he slid forward out of control, clawing wildly, until his nose bumped into the mirror on the back of the dresser. Pressed against the glass, he ceased his awkward flailing—but not for long.

As Tiger pulled himself together four eyes met—his own, and the eyes of a cat that was a stranger. At the sight of his reflection in the mirror, Tiger shot straight up in panic. He had never seen himself. With a leap, he bounded off the dresser and fled for safety under the bed. I was totally in stitches.

Over the last few weeks, I have found myself repeatedly chuckling over this incident of innocence. Tiger's reactions were so spontaneous and pure. Yet, I have come to realize that in Tiger's escapade are seen several important lessons about encountering challenges in life.

First, as Tiger perched on the side of the bed eyeing the enticing dresser top, he certainly risked failure. Indeed, I would have bet against his chances of success. Yet because he was willing to take a risk, he achieved his goal.

The willingness to take risks in life is often the only difference between success and failure. Many a gifted person has squandered his or her potential by always adopting a rule of "safety first." For without risk and challenge, none of us gives back to life all the resources and abilities God has given us.

As a teenager, the famous comedienne Minnie Pearl played the piano very well. However, she had a horror of piano recitals. She greatly feared that once she was in the public eye, she would not be able to play.

Once at a recital, she balked and refused to perform. It is reported that her mother walked quietly up to her and whispered firmly in her ear, "Don't *say* you can't play the piano. Go up to that piano and *show* them you can't play."[1]

I am convinced that God needs more people in this world who are willing to show others that they can't play the piano—and, in the process, discover that they can. God needs more Tigers who are willing to take a leap of faith and barely make it over the top. For I believe that another word for risk is *faith*.

Jesus obviously believed that His followers should be willing to accept challenges in life. In Matthew 25:14–30 Jesus tells a very interesting story about an investor who went on an extended journey and entrusted all of his financial assets to three associates. Two of the men took their share of his assets and placed them in the competitive money market so that they might accrue interest and grow. The third man, afraid of taking any risks, placed the investor's money in an insured safety deposit box. Of course, we know what happened. Months later, when the wealthy investor returned, he was delighted with the two men who had used his money to accrue dividends. However, he was furious with the man who had taken the "safety-first" philosophy and kept his money secure, but useless, in a safety deposit box.

So it is with Christian disciples today. God has given us talents to invest in the commerce of life. He certainly does not want us to place our lives in safety deposit boxes where we will never fail but, assuredly, will never succeed either. With Peter, we must have the courage to walk on the water, even if we sink. We must all listen with our spiritual ears to the challenge, "Come, follow me!" and then get out of the safety of our boats and traverse the unforeseen.

I will always be thankful for my high school debate coach, Ann Harrelson. When I was a freshman, I decided to try out for the debate team. One day it was announced that all students interested in debate should meet in Miss Harrelson's room immediately after school. With butterflies in my stomach and head bowed I slipped into her classroom and sat in the back row. When I looked up I found to my horror that most of the students trying out for the team were upper classmen and members of the Beta Club—which I certainly was not! A decision was instantly made. I was out of my league and I knew it. I stood up to leave.

As I sheepishly crept out the door, I heard Miss Harrelson's voice bark across the room, "Where are you going, young man?" Before I could answer, she emphatically said, "Please have a seat so that we can get started!" Too startled to be assertive, I sat down.

To make a long story short, I was involved with competitive debate all through high school and college. And this wonderful experience taught me the basic communication skills that I use every Sunday when I walk into the pulpit and proclaim God's word. However, I might never have had the opportunity to develop these rhetorical talents had not Miss Harrelson arrested my flight from growth when she demanded, "Where are you going, young man?" She changed my direction. She sat me down and forced me to develop God-given talents. By leading me to risk failure, she helped me to succeed.

The nineteenth-century philosopher Sydney Smith once said, "A great deal of talent is lost to the world for want of a little courage." He is absolutely right!

The primary analogy I perceived in Tiger's leap to the dresser, however, has more to do with self-discovery than with courage. When Tiger succeeded in reaching his goal, he had the unexpected experience of truly seeing himself for the very first time. He had never looked into his own eyes before he caught that glimpse of himself in the mirror.

The Danish Christian philosopher Sören Kierkegaard once wrote:

> To venture causes anxiety, but not to venture is to lose one's self . . . and to venture in the highest sense is precisely to become conscious of one's self.[2]

It is true, we will never really become conscious of who we are until we allow ourselves to cast away our moorings and venture forth on an unexplored sea. Jesus Christ stated it another way:

"For whoever wishes to save his life shall lose it; but whoever loses his life for My sake shall find it" (Matthew 16:25).

Perhaps one of the greatest yearnings in the hearts of men and women is to find themselves. And the only way to discover anything is to set out on the journey of exploration. Like Tiger, we may discover that at the summit of our goals we are not fascinated by what we originally thought we wanted. Rather, what will be truly rewarding is the self-discovery that comes in the process of making the journey. When we gaze at our own eyes in that mirror, we will see with the writer of Genesis that we are made in the image of God.

How ironic it is that in the Christian faith we gain it all by losing it all. We find security in risk. We discover ourselves when we abandon ourselves.

Sometime during our life we must risk proving to others that we can't play the piano—and in so doing discover that we can make beautiful music, the beautiful music of faith.

IIIC REFLECTIONS CIII

"Thus says the Lord . . .'Call to Me, and I will answer you, and I will tell you great and mighty things, which you do not know.' "

Jeremiah 33:2–3

But prove yourselves doers of the word, and not merely hearers who delude themselves. For if anyone is a hearer of the word and not a doer, he is like a man who looks at his natural face in the mirror; for once he has looked at himself and gone away, he has immediately forgotten what kind of person he was.

James 1:22–24

I press on in order that I may lay hold of that for which also I was laid hold of by Christ Jesus. . . . I do not regard myself as having laid hold of it yet; but one thing I do: forgetting what lies behind and reaching forward to what lies ahead, I press on toward the goal for the prize of the upward call of God in Christ Jesus.

Philippians 3:12–14

Nothing will ever be attempted, if all possible objections must first be overcome.

Samuel Johnson[3]

Not having a goal is more to be feared than not reaching a goal. . . . I would rather attempt to do something great and fail than attempt to do nothing and succeed.

Victor Frankl[4]

During the first period of a man's life the greatest danger is: not to take the risk.

Sören Kierkegaard[5]

Destiny is not a matter of chance, it is a matter of choice; it is not a thing to be waited for, it is a thing to be achieved.

William Jennings Bryan[6]

I am not going to tell you what should motivate you; whether you wish to serve God, king, country, family, political party, to work for good causes, or to fulfill your duty is up to you. I only want to show that motivation—preferably an ambition to accomplish something that really satisfies you and hurts no one—is essential.

Hans Selye[7]

DEAR FATHER:

I sometimes am confused as to whether I am afraid of failure or afraid of success. But regardless of the source of my fear, the result is the same—paralysis. Lord, free me to accept challenge in my life.

Help me to know that with every leap of faith You will place a safety net beneath me. Allow me to feel Your hand in mine when I attempt to walk on the water. And may I never forget that enough failures in the course of seeking good causes will inevitably result in victory.

In the example of Your Son, may I be a doer of Your word, and not a hearer only.

AMEN

9

ALWAYS ON TIME

I have always had a remarkable inability to memorize anything. I will never forget a face or a story, but Scripture references, telephone numbers, names, and jokes will simply not stay in my memory.

This lack of recall was particularly frustrating when I was a student. All during seminary I suffered through Greek and Hebrew. The myriad verb tenses and the noun declensions were lost to me as soon as I closed the textbook. I simply could not (or perhaps would not) commit the verb and noun endings to memory.

However, without a doubt the most uncomfortable situation that my poor memory has ever subjected me to was in a literature class when I was a junior in high school. My teacher had decided that it was not enough just to read great literary works. In addition, "gems of timeless literature" (I'll never forget that phrase!) should be committed to memory. Each student was assigned a specific "gem," which was not only to be memorized but also to be recited with appropriate inflection before the entire class. When my turn came, I was given a passage from Shakespeare's *Julius Caesar*.

Many a night I stood before the mirror in my bedroom agonizingly committing Shakespeare's phrases to memory. I would eloquently intone line after line with dramatic gestures:

> There is a tide in the affairs of men,
> Which, taken at the flood, leads on to fortune;
> Omitted, all the voyage of their life
> Is bound in shallows and in miseries.
> On such a full sea are we now afloat;
> And we must take the current when it serves,
> Or lose our ventures (IV. iii).

Well, on the great day when it came time for me to leave my classmates enthralled by a stellar performance, the tide went out and I nearly lost my venture. Only a notecard secretly taped to the top of my shoe was what got me through my ordeal, ashen-faced but intact.

The surprising thing is that now, seventeen years later, I still remember those words of the Old Bard. In fact, I not only remember them, but they come to mind quite often. Particularly during moments of major decision-making, I find myself walking the dog or staring at the moon and murmuring to myself, "There is a tide in the affairs of men, which, taken at the flood, leads on to fortune; omitted . . ." Well, that is usually as far as I can remember, but the wisdom in the passage has by then made its point. Timing—that incalculable, perplexing, and excruciating component of life—is always crucial when decisions must be made and our fate adjusted.

Unlike Brutus, in whose mouth Shakespeare put that speech, I have come to believe that timing in the life of the Christian is not due to tide or chance or fate. Rather, I believe that God works within our perceptions and our environments to direct the timing of opportunities and decisions that come our way. As such, God is the conductor of the symphony that is playing the score of our life. It is God who changes the tempo, directs the intensity, and works to keep all the contributing forces in harmony. It is our task to listen to the music and respond with readiness and sensitivity.

I remember a period in my life several years ago when I was greatly frustrated by the aspect of timing. For five years I had been an associate pastor at the First Baptist Church of Athens, Georgia, and was also coming to the completion of my doctoral studies at the University of Georgia. In short, I was ready to move on. I was tired of graduate school, I felt that I had "grown through" my role as an associate pastor, and I was eager to be the pastor of a church. Within my own perception of life's rhythm, there should have been a pastoral search committee knocking at my door.

Well, no knocks came and I was chomping at the bit. One Sunday morning as I was sitting in the worship service silently reminding God how He was forgetting about His "humble servant," Dr. J. W. Fanning, a retired vice-president of the University of Georgia and in many ways the patriarch of the church, walked to the pulpit to lead in the morning prayer. I had grown to greatly love and appreciate this man and regard him with respect. As he bowed his white head and began to pray, I found myself absorbed by his words. And then he said something that almost knocked me out of my chair.

"God, You do not always come to us when we want You to, but You are always on time." A word from God had been spoken to me through Dr. Fanning.

What God was saying to me on that day, and has reminded me of many times since, is that my perception of timing in my life and God's perception of timing *for* my life are not always the same. But God is always right. He is "always on time."

An interesting footnote to this story is that several weeks after Dr. Fanning's prayer, I was interviewed by the pastoral search committee of the First Baptist Church of Monroe, North Carolina. Weeks dragged on and I heard nothing further. As the defense of my dissertation was drawing near, I momentarily forgot about pastoral search committees and immersed myself in preparation for this event.

Finally, the dreaded day of the defense came, and I met the lions. After two hours of cross examination, I found that I had somehow passed and was released from bondage. Returning home, the first thing that I did was jump into a hot shower and start singing at the top of my lungs. And then, as it always happens, the phone rang. Jumping out of the shower without a stitch of clothes on, I huffily answered the phone. On the other end of the line, connected to a conference hookup, seven voices said "hello!" in unison. It was the pastoral search committee from Monroe asking me to accept the call to be their pastor. Suddenly feeling very exposed, I jumped under the covers of a nearby bed and tried to respond in a composed and dignified voice. Sometimes God's timing is *too* good! And sometimes I am even led to believe that God has a rich sense of humor!

As I write these words, it is several days before Christmas. I cannot help remembering the Apostle Paul's thoughts about the birth of Christ when he wrote to the church at Galatia:

> . . . we . . . were held in bondage under the elemental things of the world. But when the fulness of the time came, God sent forth His Son, born of a woman, born under the Law (Galatians 3–4:4).

The "fulness of the time"! What a wonderful phrase! How fortunate we are that God controls the timing in our universe, our world, and even in our individual lives. He always acts when the time is just right. Our task is to have the faith that He will respond to our needs and guide our decisions in the fullness of His time—the right time.

IIIꞔꞫ REFLECTIONS ꞬꞬIII

To every thing there is a season, and a time to every purpose under the heaven.

Ecclesiastes 3:1 KJV

Delight yourself in the Lord;
And He will give you the desires of your heart.

Commit your way to the Lord,
Trust also in Him, and He will do it.

Psalm 37:4–5

In all your ways acknowledge Him,
And He will make your paths straight.
Do not be wise in your own eyes;
Fear the Lord and turn away from evil.

Proverbs 3:6–7

And the Pharisees and Sadducees came up, and testing Him asked Him to show them a sign from heaven. But He answered and said to them, "When it is evening, you say, 'It will be fair weather, for the sky is red.' And in the morning, 'There will be a storm today, for the sky is red and threatening.' Do you know how to discern the appearance of the sky, but cannot discern the signs of the times?"

Matthew 16:1–3

But when He, the Spirit of truth, comes, He will guide you into all the truth.

John 16:13

A man with one watch knows what time it is; a man with two watches is never sure.

Segal's Law[1]

It sometimes happens that God leads us by an obscure intu-
ition which makes us go to a particular place without our

knowing what awaits us there. It sometimes happens, too, that he leads us by means of events that seem to have no religious significance. There is no such thing as chance.

Paul Tournier[2]

Hell is "answered" prayers. God help us if we had actually married that girl when we were twenty-one.

Lance Morrow[3]

DEAR GOD:

Please give me the gift of patience. Ever since I was a small child I have always wanted my needs fulfilled *right now!* The ability to wait, to sit quietly, to sublimate my own strong needs and impulses has never been my strength. Oh, God, when You passed out patience, You certainly overlooked me.

Yet, Father, amidst my compulsiveness, I affirm today that You are the Lord of timing. And I come again to submit the course of my life unto You. Help me to be one who does not serve two masters, but rather, with trusting restraint, one who waits upon the Lord. I know that if I synchronize my life with Your timing, I will be in step with Your will for my life. I pray this in the name of Him who questioned Your timing in Gethsemane, but who nevertheless yielded His life in total obedience, Jesus Christ, my Lord.

AMEN

10

THE GOD OF ANOTHER CHANCE

We had made the decision. The moving van was coming tomorrow. I had just signed the closing papers on our house at the lawyer's office and was walking back to the car. I looked up and there was Ed. In his sixties, retired, an avid sportsman, he had always been one of my favorites.

"Whatcha lookin' so glum about, boy?" he asked as he winked and slapped me on the shoulder.

"Well, I just sold my house and we're moving tomorrow," I replied. "Hope we're doing the right thing."

"Son, let me tell you something. You just take it from me. Don't ever look over your shoulder. And don't second guess a major decision."

His words struck home that day, and during the intervening years I have had many occasions to ponder their wisdom. Making decisions is one of the most difficult tasks an adult has to face.

Very few decisions are clear-cut, particularly the major ones. Life is just not that simple. There are always two sides to the ledger sheet, the pros and the cons. We spend days talking to friends about options, arguing every facet, turning every stone over again and again and again. And then the moment comes. A decision is at hand and we make it.

Of course, the greatest agony in making tough and debatable decisions is usually during the period of vacillation. Once the decision is made, we usually feel some relief and get on with life. But most of us have a tendency to look back periodically and say, "Did I do the right thing?"

For the Christian, the situation is even more complex because we ask God to be in on our decision-making process. As Christians, we believe that God is intimately involved in our lives and has "an opinion" about what we do. We are usually careful to try to discover what we have traditionally called "God's will for our lives," and we spend much time in prayer concerning our decisions, particularly the big ones.

I have made some decisions in my life when I was absolutely sure God and I were seeing eye to eye. There is no doubt in my mind that marrying my wife Beth not only was the right decision and within the will of God, but it was a major miracle as well. However, there have been other crucial decisions I have made when I have not felt so sure of myself. Let's be honest—it's often hard for us to distinguish between our will and God's will. And I'm not so sure that there aren't some decisions when God could be either pleased or displeased with any one option.

When it comes right down to it, perhaps the major fear lurking in our minds when we make life-changing decisions is this:

> Can I get so far off track that I can
> never get back on again? Can I miss the
> boat and never get another chance? Is it
> possible for me to diligently seek the will
> of God and really blow it?

I believe that the correct answer to these questions is "No!"

I have a firm conviction that if we conscientiously and prayerfully seek the will of God for our lives and then make an unwise decision, God is certainly not going to be stymied by our faulty decision-making process. We may live to regret aspects of the decision, but God will surely give us another chance to alter our course and make corrections.

There is a beautiful account in 1 Samuel where the Hebrews have made a series of bad decisions. Finally God comes to them—even the stern and wrathful God of the Old Testament—and says to them through His servant Samuel:

> *"Do not fear. You have committed all this evil, yet do not turn aside from following the Lord, but serve the Lord with all your heart. . . . For the Lord will not abandon His people on account of His great name, because the Lord has been pleased to make you a people for Himself"* (1 Samuel 12:20, 22).

With Samuel, I firmly believe that "the Lord will not abandon His people." God is always the God of another chance.

When we turn to the pages of the New Testament, we again find the same truth. We can see it embodied in the life of the apostle Peter, who constantly made bad decisions. But God was always faithful to work through his unwise decisions and keep Peter on course. And Peter was always faithful, despite his blunders, to try his best to follow Jesus.

While in seminary Beth and I were very prayerfully considering what we should do when I graduated. In many ways we felt that we should seek appointment as missionaries. In other ways, we both felt as if some practical experience in the pastorate should be our next step. On top of that, I was seriously considering remaining at the seminary to pursue doctoral work in New Testament studies. It seemed that our decision-making process was in a hopeless logjam, and our anxiety level was growing higher every day.

One afternoon as I pondered these options in great perplexity, I pulled a book off the shelf. It was *Thoughts in Solitude* by Thomas Merton, one of the great saints of this century. As I read the words that this contemplative monk wrote in the quietude of a monastery, I knew that the Holy Spirit was speaking to me. Merton had put into words my deepest thoughts. In one prayer he wrote:

> My Lord God, I have no idea where I am going. I do not see the road ahead of me. I cannot know for certain where it will end. Nor do I really know myself, and the fact that I

think I am following your will does not mean that I am actually doing so. But I believe that the desire to please you does in fact please you. Amen.[1]

Slowly I began to relax. I knew that even if I boarded the wrong ship, God would see that I made it to the right harbor. And now, ten years later, I know that my eventual decision to enter the pastorate was a choice that was pleasing to God.

However, at the same time that I made my decision to be a pastor, a fellow classmate in seminary, after equally prayerful consideration, decided to go to Central America as a missionary. Yet, within two years of arriving in a foreign and unfamiliar country, he realized that his greatest gifts and abilities were best used and most suitable within an American setting. Fortunately, he had the maturity to relax, complete his four-year commitment as a missionary, and immerse himself in ministry and learning in Central America. Upon completion of his commitment, he made a "course correction," returning to the United States and accepting a pastorate.

Now, as my friend surveys his life, he does not see his four years in Central America as being the result of a "bad decision," or as wasted time. Rather, he realizes, it was a period of vocational and spiritual clarification. It was a time in his life when he was able to learn many things, contribute significantly to the lives of others, and ultimately gain greater insight into himself. Once again, God does not "abandon His people." He is always the God of another chance.

And so, what about old Ed's adage to never look over your shoulder and never second-guess a major decision? Well, I'm not much on absolutes, but I think he's basically right. He's right, that is, if we've asked God to be a part of our decision and have earnestly sought to discern His will. For if we have done this, there's no need to look over our shoulder—if we do, we may lose sight of Him leading us down the road ahead.

REFLECTIONS

The steadfast of mind Thou wilt keep in perfect peace,
Because he trusts in Thee.
Trust in the Lord forever,
For in God the Lord, we have an everlasting Rock.

Isaiah 26:3–4

He said to His disciples, "Let these words sink into your ears; for the Son of Man is going to be delivered into the hands of men." . . . And it came about, when the days were approaching for His ascension, that He resolutely set His face to go to Jerusalem.

Luke 9:43–44, 51

Jesus said to him, "No one, after putting his hand to the plow and looking back, is fit for the Kingdom of God."

Luke 9:62

Jesus, crying out with a loud voice, said, "Father, into Thy hands I commit My spirit."

Luke 23:46

But if any of you lacks wisdom, let him ask of God, who gives to all men generously and without reproach, and it will be given to him. But let him ask in faith without any doubting, for the one who doubts is like the surf of the sea driven and tossed by the wind.

James 1:5–6

I don't know Who—or what—put the question, I don't know when it was put. I don't even remember answering. But at some moment I did answer Yes to Someone—or Something—and from that hour I was certain that existence is meaningful and that, therefore, my life, in self-surrender, had a goal.

From that moment I have known what it means "not to look back," and "to take no thought for the morrow."

Dag Hammarskjöld[2]

If you slip and stumble and forget God for an hour, and assert your old proud self, and rely upon your own clever wisdom, don't spend too much time in anguished regrets and self-accusations but begin again, just where you are.

Thomas R. Kelly[3]

God often gives in one brief moment that which he has for a long time denied.

Thomas à Kempis[4]

DEAR FATHER:

I most earnestly seek to do Your will in my life. Yet, if I am honest, I often cannot clearly discern Your leading. Maybe it's my spiritual blindness and insensitivity. Maybe You are deliberate in Your opaqueness. But whatever the cause or reason, Lord, I often do not know what Your will for my life truly is.

Still, decisions must be made and forks in the road chosen. Help me to always seek to discover what You would have me do. And then give me the courage to proceed in all confidence knowing that You are always the Lord of another chance. You will not desert me. You will be faithful to lead me to green pastures and still waters if I but seek to follow You.

AMEN

SHALLOWS OF
DEPRESSION,
ANGER, AND
HELPLESSNESS

11

TWO QUARTS LOW

Depression is one of the most common maladies that afflicts the human race. Of course, we are all "blue" at times. But, within a day or two, we usually return to normal and our old spark is back. However, depression of a deeper and more debilitating type is also very common and cannot be dismissed so easily with a "you'll get over it tomorrow" attitude.

It is estimated that at least 50 percent of Americans experience varying levels of depression on a recurrent basis. In addition, one out of ten will experience depression in one of its more severe forms within his or her lifetime.[1] As surely as we will catch the common cold, all of us will also experience the throes of depression, either within ourselves or within one we love.

The symptoms of depression are myriad. Physically, we may experience lethargy, unrelenting fatigue, headaches, vertigo, loss of appetite, lack of sexual interest, and a host of other somatic reactions. Emotionally, we may become despondent, pessimistic, and either weep frequently or wish that we could. And spiritually, for weeks on end we often feel that God is far away from us. Frequently, we begin to fear that if the depression does not lift, it will destroy us. We will have a nervous breakdown or go crazy or commit suicide. And so we deepen our depression by worrying about our depression. We feel like a person sunk to the waist in quicksand who, with every struggle to get out, becomes mired deeper and deeper. We want to go to sleep and not wake up until it's all over.

I have experienced depression from time to time in my own life and fully expect that I will deal with it again during future transitions and struggles. However, in continuing to learn to cope more effectively with depression's depleting powers, I have formed two "mental pictures." When depression begins to sap my vital energies, I brush the dust from them and get them out to reflect on. I share these two pictures with you, because I believe that you can gain some helpful insights into the cause and prevention of depression.

The first mental picture is really a story from my high school days. I grew up in a small, Southern town, and there was not much for energetic teenage boys to do at night. On cold winter evenings, I would often go with several of my friends to a small gas station located on the edge of the Atlanta highway. Perched on Coke crates and sitting around a kerosene heater, we would tell jokes, spin yarns, shoot the bull, and while the night away.

One evening I was in the station when a very pretty but agitated young woman careened her car into the lot and quickly jumped out. With my curiosity naturally aroused, I walked outside with the station mechanic to offer her assistance. An interesting conversation ensued.

"Can I help you, ma'am?" the mechanic asked.

"I sure hope so. Something's wrong with the heat gauge on my dashboard. It keeps lighting up, flickering on and off. Can you fix the gauge? It's driving me crazy!"

"Well, let me see," the mechanic drawled. Spitting out his tobacco juice, he opened the hood.

Several minutes elapsed. Then he closed the hood and sauntered up to the driver's window.

"Ain't nothing wrong with your heat gauge, ma'am. It's working just fine."

"Whatcha mean there's nothing wrong with the gauge? It keeps blinking on and off," she replied testily.

"Well, like I said, ma'am, there ain't nothing wrong with the gauge. The problem is you're two quarts low on oil."

With that I turned and walked inside, attempting to stifle

my laughter. A humorous parody on life had transpired before my eyes.

What does the gas station story have to do with depression? I believe a great deal! Depression is the heat gauge on our emotional dashboard. And when stress of any kind causes our psychic and emotional systems to overheat, then depression kicks in and we receive a warning that something is wrong.

The heat gauge in a car can blink on for multiple reasons—a low water level in the radiator, a leaking radiator hose, a faulty thermostat, insufficient oil, a hole in the oil pan, etc. Likewise, the emotional indicator of depression can flicker on in our lives due to multiple causes, such as repressed anger, grief, guilt, helplessness, a significant loss, or even a significant success. In addition, there can be physical causes, such as hormonal changes, blood sugar imbalance, menstruation, or thyroid malfunction, just to name a few. The point is that the depression, with all its disturbing symptoms and resultant fears is *not* what we should be concerned about. Rather, we should direct our attention to the *cause* of the depression. When two quarts of oil were added to the young woman's engine, her heat gauge light dimmed out. And when we discover the stressor that is plaguing us and effectively deal with it, our depression will go away as well.

I have found that in my own life the two most common causes of depression are repressed anger and a feeling of helplessness. In the next two chapters I will address these two factors directly. However, for now I would like to share with you another mental picture that has helped me recognize more easily the embers of anger or the paralysis of helplessness in my life.

Several years ago I was having lunch with a gifted psychotherapist. As we conversed, I shared with him that I was feeling some nagging symptoms of depression. After listening to more than just my words, he said, ''I intuitively sense that you are intensely angry at something or with somebody. I'm not sure what it is, but I feel that you should discover why you're so angry.'' At first I dismissed my friend's hunch as being farfetched. I didn't feel the least bit angry with anybody. In fact, I didn't feel that much of anything. I just had a good case of the "blahs."

Later that evening, however, I found myself sitting alone in the den in front of our blazing fireplace. I had come home very late, following yet another meeting, and discovered that Beth had already gone to bed. All was quiet. In the stillness I began to think about the psychotherapist's comments. I knew that according to Freud, depression is primarily caused by anger that is not directed toward its proper object but rather is "swallowed"—not expressed—and turned inward to be transformed into depression. Yet, even though I sensed Freud was correct, I was struggling to discern the reason for my anger.

As the fire crackled and popped, I looked across at a vacant chair opposite me. Suddenly and spontaneously I created a scenario in which I personified anger. I asked "Mr. Anger" to come in our front door and sit in the chair. Rather than treat him as an enemy, I decided to talk with him as a friend. I said something like this:

> "Okay, Mr. Anger, I'm not going to be scared of you any longer. I know you're not my enemy, you're my friend. Now tell me, what is it that we need to deal with? Why am I so angry and so unable to express it? What have you come to tell me?"

I thought about how Beth had probably been lonely when she went to bed. I looked at my plate of cold food still sitting on the table. Slowly it began to dawn on me: I was angry because in recent months I, as a minister, was being inundated by the legitimate needs of people I loved. But because I was dutifully responding to their need, I was also frequently neglecting my own family and my own needs. I hadn't had a day off in weeks. I knew that I was not being a very good husband. And yet, when Mrs. Smith called and told me that Mrs. Jones "needs a visit," how could I tell her no, much less express to her my frustration and anger? Suddenly a feeling of true rage welled up inside me. I had discovered the source of my depression! I was angry at an overload of demands from good people that I loved, and I had not known how to express my feelings.

To make a long story short, I decided to deal with my anger by taking my calendar the very next day and marking one day off in every week through the remainder of the year. I cut out unnecessary meetings. I canceled some engagements. And I also began to make myself say no when appropriate. I did not pop my cork and fly off the handle at the next person who called me. But I did take definite action to put "two quarts of oil" back into my emotional engine.

The point I am making is that when we become depressed, instead of running away from the emotion or flailing away in quicksand, we must instead sit quietly by the fire and ask, "Why am I depressed?" Invite Mr. Anger, or Mrs. Grief, or Dr. Guilt to sit down and talk with you. And talk aloud. Don't be afraid to ramble. If your spouse wakes up and hears you, or a friend walks in on you, he or she might think you are crazy. But in actuality, it might be the sanest thing you've done in a long time.

All of us need fireside chats from time to time. We need to take our emotions seriously and welcome them into our midst. If we bar the door to our feelings and refuse to listen to what they are telling us, then we will become depressed. I don't know about you, but I'd rather talk to an empty chair any day than suffer the agony of depression.

ⅢⅢ REFLECTIONS ⅢⅢ

Be gracious to me, O Lord, for I am pining away;
Heal me, O Lord, for my bones are dismayed.
And my soul is greatly dismayed;
But Thou, O Lord—how long?

. . .

I am weary with my sighing;
Every night I make my bed swim,

I dissolve my couch with my tears.
My eye has wasted away with grief;
It has become old because of all my adversaries.

Psalm 6:2–3, 6–7

Why are you in despair, O my soul?
And why have you become disturbed within me?
Hope in God, for I shall yet praise Him,
The help of my countenance, and my God.

Psalm 42:11

"Is the Lord not in Zion? Is her King not within her?"
. . .
I mourn, dismay has taken hold of me.
Is there no balm in Gilead?
Is there no physician there?
Why then has not the health of the daughter of my people
*   been restored?*

Jeremiah 8:19, 21–22

"Blessed are those who mourn, for they shall be comforted."

Matthew 5:4

At that time Jesus . . . said, . . . "Come to Me, all who are
weary and heavy-laden, and I will give you rest. Take My
yoke upon you, and learn from Me, for I am gentle and
humble in heart; and you shall find rest for your souls. For
My yoke is easy, and My load is light."

Matthew 11:25, 28–30

He who wants to enjoy the glory of the sunrise must live through the night.

Anonymous

In the midst of winter, I finally learned that there was in me an invincible summer.

Albert Camus[2]

DEAR LORD:

I am depressed today. Life feels very heavy. And, if I am honest, I must admit that my depression scares me. It frightens me because I feel like I am losing control. I anxiously react as if a masked man has grabbed me from behind and is trying to pin me down—to rob me, to steal from me the energy of life, to kill me.

Father, help me not to fear the depression but rather to listen to its muffled voice. Help me to understand why I am depressed and then to have the courage to do something about it.

Even though it is difficult, I thank You today for depression. For like a fever that burns in one's body seeking to purify infirmity, I know that my depression is trying to cleanse my soul of grief, anger, or guilt. Grant unto me the strength to persevere and the courage to be honest with myself. Through Jesus Christ, my Lord.

AMEN

12

BE ANGRY, BUT DO NOT SIN

If unexpressed anger is often transformed within us into debilitating depression, how can we learn to communicate our wrath in a mature and constructive manner? This is a question that daily perplexes us all.

In my own dealing with the problem of the expression of anger, I have frequently turned to Paul's Letter to the Ephesians for reflection and guidance. In Ephesians 4:26–27 (RSV), Paul states:

> Be angry, but do not sin; do not let the sun go down on your anger.

In this simple admonition, Paul presents three very important axioms concerning anger that Christians should understand and to which they should adhere.

The first thing Paul says is *"Be angry."* In other words, that feisty little apostle is advocating that it is perfectly permissible, normal, and healthy for Christians to become angry and to express their irritations and frustrations to one another.

Modern psychologists are in agreement with the thinking of the apostle Paul. Erik Erikson, one of the world's leading theorists in the area of developmental psychology, blames the failure to achieve intimacy in our age on the inability of people to engage with their anger and express their frustrations to one another. Erikson has correctly perceived that the repression of anger has also caused the repression of other important interpersonal emotions, such as kindness, empathy, and affection.

As a pastor and a counselor, I can say without reservation that I have seen far more lives crippled and marriages wither because of the repression of anger than from its expression. People simply cannot be happy together and foster deep intimacy until they can develop ways to be comfortable in expressing their tempers with one another. Anger can, and should, be a form of intimacy.

Recently I preached a sermon on the topic of anger in which I stressed that it is all right for Christians to express anger in a mature fashion to one another. Unknown to me, a psychiatrist was visiting our church that Sunday. On Monday morning I received a phone call from this Christian doctor asking me if I would visit the public mental health center and sit in on a group therapy session he was leading. I told him I would be glad to.

On the day of the group therapy session I arrived a few minutes early to be briefed by the doctor. He told me several of his patients were suffering emotional problems that were primarily due to repressed anger. These same patients also professed to be Christians and felt that their faith commitment did not allow for them to express anger.

As the therapy session began, I quickly noticed a young woman in her thirties sitting withdrawn in a corner. She was pale and obviously depressed. As the doctor introduced me and asked me to share a few thoughts concerning the relationship between Christian faith and the expression of anger, this young woman began to perk up and pay attention.

To make a long story short, she had been recently separated from her husband and was awaiting the divorce process. For the last five years she had been intermittently depressed, often severely, and her depression had greatly inhibited her ability to contribute to a healthy marriage. Her depression was directly related to a turbulent childhood in which she had been frequently and justifiably angered. Yet her mother had squelched her expression of anger by telling her that "good Christians always turn the other cheek."

As the session continued, it became obvious that I was the first "reverend," as she called me, to give her permission to release some of the anger she held within. The fact that she could be a devout Christian and honestly express anger seemed to be a new revelation to her.

About a year later, I received a letter from this same woman. She had been reunited with her husband, her depression was greatly improved, and her marriage was returning to health. She stated that the beginning of her progress came when she realized that as a Christian she had "permission to get angry." When she began to express her anger, her depression began to lift and intimacy began to be restored to her marriage.

I believe that the example of Jesus Christ, as well as Paul's admonition to "be angry," do give to Christians the permission not only to feel the natural emotion of anger but to express it as well. Yet we must also address the question of "How?" How can we express our anger in a mature way so that it is a positive and unifying force rather than a negative and destructive emotion?

The apostle Paul addresses the issue of *how* to express anger when he states, *"Be angry, but do not sin."* A healthy approach to communicating anger is found in the four short words, "but do not sin."

What is sin? At its most basic level, sin is any action, emotion, or attitude that separates us from God, ourselves, or other people. The account of the first occurrence of sin in the Genesis story clearly tells us that sin is an action that results in relational separation. As a result of their attitude and action, Adam and Eve were separated from God. They put on clothes to symbolize an emerging breach in their own marriage relationship. And finally, they were even separated from Eden, their source of rootedness in life.

Now I believe that when the apostle Paul states that we should be angry but not sin, he is saying that it is all right to express our anger if we do not allow it to result in relational separation. Anger must be used to bind us together and not tear us apart.

Anger is a two-sided emotion that can be compared to nitroglycerin. Nitroglycerin in the proper dosage can be a tremendously helpful drug for relieving pain and restoring circulation to the hearts of angina victims. In the same way anger can be used to remove pain in relationships, stimulate our hearts, and aid the circulation of intimacy. However, nitroglycerin, when used in large amounts, can also be transformed into dynamite. And the destructive power of dynamite maims, kills, and destroys. Likewise, anger, when totally unbridled and used irresponsibly, can literally blow relationships apart.

I believe that Paul, a man who certainly had a fiery temper, is saying in effect: "If you get angry, be responsible for your anger. Don't just blow your top like a keg of dynamite and walk away leaving relationships in shambles. If you express your anger and, as a result, a breach in relationships results, you have a responsibility to restore healing and health to that relationship. Do not allow your anger to separate you from another."

As I write these words, I am reminded of an episode that transpired recently in my own life. After an unusually exhausting day, I crept wearily home seeking peace and quiet, only to find that my two boys had missed their naps, were irritable, and were demanding attention. When my four-year-old son, Drew, knocked his one-year-old brother, Luke, down some steps, my anger spilled over. I exploded and began to act like a four-year-old myself. Jerking Drew up, I belligerently carried him to his room. With eyes glaring I told him not to come out of his room until I gave him permission. Turning around, with a self-righteous air, I firmly—very firmly—shut the door.

As the door slammed, I knew that I had blown it. Not that I was wrong in getting angry, but that, because of a frustrating day, I had dumped all of my pent-up hostility upon my little son. I walked out to the backyard and sat down under an oak tree, feeling miserable.

After I had cooled off, I trudged back upstairs, opened the

door to my son's room, and sat down on the bed where he was lying. I picked him up, held him, and said: ''Drew, it wasn't good for you to knock Luke down the steps. That could really hurt him. And that's why I made you come to your room. Do you understand?''

Very dejectedly, Drew nodded his head and looked down at the floor.

''But,'' I continued, ''Daddy is also sorry that he treated you like that. I shouldn't have yelled at you and jerked you up. That's wrong. I had a hard day today and I lost my temper. I'm really sorry. Do you think you can forgive Daddy?''

Well, Drew began to smile. With a twinkle in his blue eyes and with the pride of a kindergartner who has just learned a new word, he chirped, ''You're an old grouch!''

I laughed with a true sense of forgiven joy and we hugged each other. Suddenly I heard a little voice say, ''Let's play blocks.'' A tired old grouch was now ready to sprawl on the floor and relax with his son. Anger that could have led to relational separation had resulted in the deepening of intimacy.

Why? It was because I chose to return to my son's room and attempt to heal our relationship before the wounds I had inflicted with my anger had had time to fester. As Paul states, I did not let the sun go down on my anger.

Quite simply, Paul is saying that when we express anger and a rift is created in a relationship, we should not sit around for very long hoping that the relational chasm will be bridged by the passage of time. Rather, we must quickly take the initiative to build bridges and mend fences and talk through our problems.

Now, I do not believe that we should take Paul absolutely literally when he says not to ''let the sun go down. . . .'' If you need a day or two to simmer and gain perspective on a situation, take the time to do so. But don't allow a week or a month to go by. Don't forget about it and hope it will go away. Anger will not go away. Rather, an angry exchange left jagged and unresolved will only eat away at the roots of friendship and fondness. We must move with deliberate haste to make amends with our brother or sister. For time is of the essence in determining whether the expression of anger will lead to the deepening of intimacy or the broadening of separation.

After long years of interpersonal struggle with the likes of hardheaded Peter, holier-than-thou James, turn-tail John Mark, and above all himself—bombastic Paul—the great apostle had learned a few things about anger. He did not write much about it. But when he did address the issue, he succinctly put it all in a nutshell. *"Be angry, but do not sin; do not let the sun go down on your anger."* These are hard-earned words for the wise.

⠸⠿ REFLECTIONS ⠿⠸

Like a city that is broken into and without walls is a man who has no control over his spirit.

Proverbs 25:28

Faithful are the wounds of a friend.

Proverbs 27:6

"If therefore you are presenting your offering at the altar, and there remember that your brother has something against you, leave your offering there before the altar, and go your way; first be reconciled to your brother, and then come and present your offering."

Matthew 5:23–24

And he entered again into a synagogue; and a man was there with a withered hand. And they [the Pharisees] were watching

Him to see if He would heal him on the Sabbath, in order that they might accuse Him. . . . And after looking around at them with anger, grieved at their hardness of heart, He said to the man, "Stretch out your hand." And he stretched it out, and his hand was restored.

Mark 3:1–2, 5

And the Passover of the Jews was at hand, and Jesus went up to Jerusalem. And He found in the temple those who were selling oxen and sheep and doves, and the moneychangers seated. And He made a scourge of cords, and drove them all out of the temple, with the sheep and oxen; and He poured out the coins of the moneychangers, and overturned their tables.

John 2:13–15

Let all bitterness and wrath and anger and clamor and slander be put away from you, along with all malice. And be kind to one another, tender-hearted, forgiving each other, just as God in Christ also has forgiven you.

Ephesians 4:31–32

Everyone who hates his brother is a murderer.

1 John 3:15

Anyone can become angry—that is easy, but to be angry with the right person, to the right degree, at the right time, for the right purpose, and in the right way—this is difficult.

Aristotle[1]

Anger may repast with thee for an hour, but not repose with thee for a night; the continuance of anger is hatred, the continuance of hatred turns malice. That anger is not warrantable which hath seen two suns.

Francis Quarles[2]

Anger is one of the sinews of the soul; he that wants [lacks] it hath a maimed mind.

Thomas Fuller[3]

> *I was angry with my friend*
> *I told my wrath, my wrath did end.*
> *I was angry with my foe:*
> *I told it not, my wrath did grow.*

William Blake[4]

Anger is never sudden. It is born of a long, prior irritation that has ulcerated the spirit and built up an accumulation of force that results in an explosion. It follows that a fine outburst of rage is by no means a sign of a frank, direct nature.

Cesare Pavese[5]

DEAR GOD:

As I kneel to pray the sun is setting. There are but minutes left in the day. Give me the courage to go in haste and say to my friend, "I am angry and we must talk. But first, be assured that I love you."

AMEN

13

LIVING IN BABYLON

I have a friend who, at the age of fifty-five, lost his job due to no fault of his own. Over the ensuing weeks, Jack became severely depressed. His job had been the central focus of his life, and now he felt completely adrift.

Jack began working with his company as soon as he returned from the Korean War. At age twenty, he started at the bottom, and over the years worked his way up to the senior managerial staff. For thirty-five years, he poured his life and soul into the company—and then the sand castle crumbled. Because of the change in the economy, new technological innovations, and some bad business investments, the company slid into bankruptcy. Jack came to work one morning as he had done for thirty-five years and was asked to clean out his desk. It was all over.

After wading in despondency for several months, Jack came to talk with me about feeling depressed. He had recently consulted his doctor. After a thorough physical, he had been pronounced in good health, yet the depression would not lift. He dreaded getting up in the morning, couldn't bring himself to do anything around the house, and was extremely moody. As the days went by he felt increasingly alone and fearful that the depression would never leave.

As we talked, several reasons for Jack's state of depression became quickly apparent. He was intensely angry that his company had folded. Yet he had found no way to express that anger. He was simply turning his fury in on himself, with the result that it was transformed into depression.

Jack was also grieving because a comfortable and fulfilling livelihood had suddenly "died." He was having to say good-bye to a way of life, to colleagues, to dreams, and to a future he had planned. He was in an agony of grief, yet there was no funeral to attend, no place to bury the body, no way to walk away from the graveyard and begin anew. Jack kept his sorrow festering inside.

But Jack was overcome by more than anger and grief. He also felt a tremendous sense of helplessness. He did not want to retire. Sitting around the house drove him crazy. Yet at age fifty-five, he was finding that other companies did not want to hire and train him because he would be retiring within ten years. He was in a vocational quandary. When the loss of a job, unyielding depression, and inability to find new employment are combined, the result is a man who feels powerless to change his situation and get on with his life.

Time and again I have seen the issue of helplessness become one of the major contributors to depression. And I have found that if people can be led to see that they are not helpless, that they do have power over their lives, then the fog of their depression begins to lift and evaporate.

Whenever I begin to be overcome by a feeling of help-lessness in my own life and find depression creeping in on me, I recall a story about one of my seminary professors. Dr. Hugo Culpepper was a young missionary in the Philippines at the outbreak of World War II. When the Japanese invaded the islands, he was arrested and ordered to report to a prison camp. Each internee was allowed to take into the camp only what he could personally carry.

Dr. Culpepper knew that the war might drag on for a very long time. He was aware that, under the harsh prison rules, he would be helpless in many ways. Any food that he took with him would be quickly eaten. Any luxury items would be soon expended. So when Dr. Culpepper walked through the prison gates, he carried two books under his arm—a Greek New Testament, and a Greek lexicon. He had decided that during the long months of internment he would teach himself to read Greek and broaden his knowledge of the New Testament.

This story has always had symbolic implications for me because Dr. Culpepper was a man who refused to become helpless. His captors might imprison his body but they couldn't control his mind. So the long hours of waiting for liberation were turned into positive and useful days of study, preparing to teach future seminary students such as myself. Hugo Culpepper found a way of turning depressing circumstances into a positive situation. He took charge of his life.

Hundreds of years ago, the prophet Jeremiah found himself in similar circumstances. Jerusalem had fallen to Nebuchadnezzar, and hundreds of Israelites were ripped from their homes and taken captive to Babylon. Depression was rampant as a sense of uprootedness and helplessness pervaded the people. It was at this moment that God spoke to his prophet Jeremiah and told him to proclaim this message to his people:

> *"Thus says the Lord of hosts, the God of Israel, to all the exiles whom I have sent into exile from Jerusalem to Babylon, 'Build houses and live in them; and plant gardens, and eat their produce. Take wives and become the fathers of sons and daughters, and take wives for your sons and give your daughters to husbands, that they may bear sons and daughters; and multiply there and do not decrease. And seek the welfare of the city where I have sent you unto exile, and pray to the Lord on its behalf; for in its welfare you will have welfare.'"* (29:4–7).

In effect, God was saying to His people, "In the midst of your helplessness, take charge of your lives. Do something creative and positive with what is yours to control."

And so, what happened to Jack? After skating on the ice for a little longer, he did decide to take charge of what he could control. He had always liked restoring antiques, but in recent years had had little time for this source of enjoyment. Now Jack decided that he would open an antique shop where he could refinish and sell furniture. He and his wife had always wanted to travel. So now they take long weekend trips and go wherever their hearts desire. Although Jack still misses his previous job and wrestles with the task of having to reshape his life's dream, his depression has greatly lifted. And when those feelings of despondency occasionally return, Jack goes out and sands and scrapes furniture. In the midst of his Babylon, he is building a new house, planting a nourishing garden, and enjoying his children. He has refused to be helpless any longer. With God's strength, he is taking charge of his life and overcoming depression.

ⅢＣ❑ REFLECTIONS ❑ＣⅢ

Why is light given to him who suffers,
And life to the bitter of soul . . . ?
Why is light given to a man whose way is hidden,
And whom God has hedged in?

Job 3:20, 23

Hear my cry, O God;
Give heed to my prayer.
From the end of the earth I call to Thee, when my heart is
    faint;
Lead me to the rock that is higher than I.

Psalm 61:1–2

But Zion said, ''The Lord has forsaken me,
And the Lord has forgotten me.''
''Can a woman forget her nursing child,
And have no compassion on the son of her womb?
Even these may forget, but I will not forget you.
Behold, I have inscribed you on the palms of My hands.''

Isaiah 49:14–16a

"Ask, and it shall be given to you; seek, and you shall find; knock, and it shall be opened to you."

                                                          Matthew 7:7

Not that I speak from want; for I have learned to be content in whatever circumstances I am.

                                                          Philippians 4:11

I believe that cure for depression occurs when the individual comes to believe that he is not helpless and that an individual's susceptibility to depression depends on the success or failure of his previous experience with controlling his environment.

                                                     Martin E. P. Seligman[1]

I cannot choose my circumstances, but I can choose my attitudes.

                                                          Anonymous

DEAR LORD:

As I walked to work today, I must have appeared stooped, I was so weighed down with worry and helplessness. There are just so many things going on in my life right now that I feel powerless to control—events and decisions that will shape my future and affect my family in so many ways.

And then, standing on a street corner lost in thought, the memory flooded back. I was sitting in the kitchen of my childhood eating cereal at the family table. And there on the wall hung the yellow ceramic plaque I haven't seen

in years. I don't know who wrote the words but the green
letters read:

> Grant me the serenity to accept things
> I cannot change, courage to
> change things I can, and wisdom to
> know the difference.[2]

God, that's my prayer today. These words from childhood
say all that I feel. Grant unto me this serenity, courage, and
wisdom.

AMEN

REEFS OF DEATH AND SORROW

14

DEATH IN THE MIDST OF LIFE

The Episcopal rector had asked me to assist him with a funeral, and I was sitting in my study becoming familiar with the graveside service in the *Book of Common Prayer*. As I read the beautiful words of the service, I came to a sentence that pricked my curiosity. "In the midst of life we are in death; in whom may we seek succour, but of Thee, O Lord?" I read these cryptic words several times, sensing that here was a truth I could not fully fathom.

Over the intervening weeks, I often found myself silently repeating the phrase, "In the midst of life we are in death." It has become for me a spiritual riddle to unravel, and I am only now beginning to comprehend the mystery. Perhaps I can best express my emerging understanding of these words by relating a story of a man named Bob who struggled desperately with the aura of death.

Death first came upon Bob when he was twenty years old and in the midst of life. He was a raw recruit in an army basic training camp. With shaved head and aching muscles, he was learning to fire a rifle, lob grenades, and thrust a bayonet into the straw stomach of a yet unseen enemy. In the quiet nights when exhaustion overcame his soldier's composure, the boy within him wondered if a bayonet might not one day slash through his own body. He dismissed death, however, in the solace of sleep.

The war mercifully ended before bayonet dummies became

warm flesh. With joyous relief, Bob returned to Georgia—to the farm, the red soil, and to the girl he loved. At the age of twenty-one, he married and settled down to actualize what he considered to be the virtues of adulthood—seriousness, sobriety, intensity, and long hours of work. He began successfully to sell automobiles, the passion of his life, and consequently became a respected businessman in his community.

By the time he was thirty, he had three children to feed and to love. Despite the newness of birth, however, life was somehow becoming an ever duller routine of rushing to work in the morning and dragging home in the evening to encounter childish quarreling, snotty noses, and an exhausted wife. Sweethearts had become parents, parents had become providers, and providers were becoming weary. In the midst of life something had begun to die.

Bob knew that things were not right. The zest of his life was dissolving. Youthfulness disappeared before the mirror. He admitted to a creeping distance between himself and his wife. He felt increasingly depressed, stifled, and trapped. Although he was a steward in the Methodist church, he knew that his spiritual moorings were coming untied.

As Bob tried to cope with his increasing awareness of mortality, he began to entertain fleeting fantasies of escape—hopping a freight to California, having a wild affair, winning a lottery and becoming immeasurably wealthy. And although he wanted desperately to talk to someone, to open up his darkness to light, he felt that his fears and fantasies were too earthy to discuss with his minister. They were also far too threatening and revealing to share with his wife. Consequently, the one person with whom he spent most of the hours of his day became a safe and sympathetic ear of comfort—his secretary. And sympathy became sensuality. Sensuality became infatuation. Good sense became poor judgment, and the way of all flesh was trodden.

As he lay remorsefully in a squeaking bed on a humid summer night, the moment came when Bob finally determined to cease trying to escape the presence of death. He decided to face its snare. Snuffing out his cigarette, he put on his clothes in the darkness and drove home to confess all to his wife. Between the sobs, the accusations, and the pain, he spoke of how the affair meant nothing, of how he was trying desperately to feel alive again, young again, attractive once more. But, unfortunately, she neither understood nor forgave. She ordered him out of the house and bolted the door.

For six months Bob lived in the local hotel, seeing on weekends the children he dearly loved. Occasionally he would despondently drink too much and recklessly drive to his home to plead and pound on the locked door and rattle the pinned windows. The separation from his wife, his children, his God, and himself was devouring him. The hotel became a prison, a torture chamber.

Finally, in anger and desperation, fantasy became reality. Selling his business partnership and loading his car with suitcases full of nothing, he drove with his secretary from Georgia to Nevada to obtain a legal divorce. He wanted desperately to see if life could begin again in another world. Perhaps he could forget it all, leave it all, and start anew.

Bob threw himself relentlessly into new work. Although death's nagging aura followed him to Nevada, he numbed himself to its lure through long days of labor. Within ten years, he had acquired one of the largest Cadillac dealerships in Nevada. Yet, although he had achieved business success, peace eluded him. At night, he would escape death by drinking and going to the casinos. He would lose a week's full earnings in a brief hour at a blackjack table. And when a friend would drive him home in a drunken stupor, he would, through thickened lips, endlessly repeat the names of his children. In attempting to elude death, Bob was rushing full circle into death's embrace.

When he was fifty-two, a telegram came one day to his office. It was from his daughter. The last time he had seen her was when she was seven. And now she informed him that she had given birth to a baby boy. Something broke loose inside him. For once, there was an authentic and spontaneous burst of joy. Life was beginning again. A new generation was born. Somehow, somewhere, there was another chance to set it all right.

Bob did not like to fly. So he hurriedly bought a train

ticket and, before inhibitions could overcome him, he set off across the continent to hold his grandson in his arms. Somewhere along the way, however, he stopped to change trains. Walking across a sleet-covered station platform at night, he slipped and fell, brutally banging his head against the pavement. A total stranger to those about him, he drifted anonymously into a coma. Death came at last.

There is something about this story that frightens and haunts me. The sheer tragedy of the story is frightening. But more than being frightened, I have always been haunted by this account because Bob was my grandfather, and I was the baby he longed to see. For me, this drama is not just a hypothetical situation, another's misfortune that couldn't happen to me. No, Bob is the flesh of my flesh, the blood of my blood. And if we are honest, we must admit that we all share a kinship with Bob somewhere in our being.

What do we all have in common with my grandfather? We are all tempted to try to escape death in the midst of life—to deny that we are getting older, that there are things dying within us all the time. We all desperately want to avoid grief—to say no goodbyes, to burn no bridges, to leave the doors wide open to all our options. And it is this desire within us, the desire to escape death, that is one of Satan's prime instruments in steering us toward spiritual destruction.

Somehow we must come to see that no one is immune to death's subtle seduction. For we are all vulnerable to the lure of believing that if we can only win the promotion, gain notoriety, run a marathon, write a book, crawl into bed with the infatuation of the moment, or work ourselves into numbness—*then* we will be conquering life, sustaining youth, reversing decline, defeating death. We are like a herd of wild buffalo fleeing from diversionary prairie fires set by crafty Indian hunters. Although we may be successfully fleeing from the fire, we are unknowingly rushing pell-mell toward a deadly cliff. In fleeing the flash points of life, we set ourselves on a course that will plummet us to sure destruction.

Today, I wish that my grandfather could have said to his wife rather than to his secretary, "Honey, something is dying inside me. I am having feelings I don't understand. I'm afraid! I'm frightened! Let's leave the kids with your mother and go away for a few days. We need to talk. To be together again.'' I wish he had consulted his minister, a trusted friend, and not a bottle of whiskey. Yet because my grandfather was far more interested in fleeing from death than in facing it head-on, he forsook the very ones who could have helped him and fled with his secretary toward the cliffs of Nevada. How strange it is, that if we flee death, we die. If we face death, we live again.

And so, in the midst of life, how can we face our death and begin to make our peace? I assure you that I do not have all the answers to this question. Indeed, I hold very few in my searching hands. For in the midst of my life, I, like my grandfather, am struggling with death, seeking to make my own peace. However, in my struggle I have discovered several life-rails that have so far kept me from falling into calamity.

First, I have come to see that we cannot truly live to our *fullest potential* until we have somehow encountered the reality of our own impending death. This truth was vividly brought home to me when I read a biography of one of my favorite novelists, James Michener. The author, John P. Hayes, depicts a time when Michener was forced to confront his own death. The result of this encounter was a positive turning point in his life.

When World War II began, Michener was thirty-six years old and an editor for a publishing company. Although he grappled daily with the writings of other people, he had yet to write his first novel. With the Japanese attack on Pearl Harbor, he responded to a patriotic urge, joined the navy, and was assigned to a supply base in the South Pacific.

One night Michener found himself as a passenger on a transport plane flying over a vast expanse of the ocean. Suddenly the plane's engines sputtered and lost power. With difficulty, the plane managed to limp back to New Caledonia. However, as the plane was crossing the coastline, it began to vibrate violently and plummet out of control. With every plunging second, death became more certain. At the last possible moment the frantic pilot was able to bring the plane out of the dive and crash-land on an airstrip.

Although Michener was not hurt, he was greatly shaken. Years later, he recounted to John Hayes that this moment of facing his mortality was critical to his future and to the literary success of his life. From that moment on, as Hayes states:

> death meant nothing at all. . . . He feared nothing ahead of him; and he left nothing behind. . . . Some internal voice that night told Michener he was a better man than the navy or the publishing business or the universities had ever known, and all of a sudden he wanted so much more. He had nothing to prove to anyone but himself, and he wanted to prove himself as a writer. In the final analysis he did not want to fail for having never tried.[1]

As a result of his facing death, Michener was compelled to write. Consequently, he has become one of America's most successful novelists.

Undoubtedly, there is something about encountering the reality of our own impending death that can catapult us into experiencing a richer and more productive level of life. For Michener, death slapped him in the face and awakened him to say "What can I lose? I always wanted to write and I nearly missed my chance. I think I'll try."

For a business executive totally held captive by his work until a heart attack nearly released him from all of life, the monologue might be: "For all these years I thought the bottom line of the ledger sheet was so important. Now I know it wasn't. Lying in the intensive care ward struggling for breath, I suddenly knew that what I really wanted was more time with my family, more afternoons to play golf, and just some days to sit in the sun."

And yet, do we have to be almost killed in a plane crash or suffer a heart attack to face our death and gain a new perspective on life? I certainly hope not. I believe that we can be healthily brought to a deeper level of life by deliberately taking our own death seriously—by firmly, but without morbidity, reminding ourselves that life cannot be taken for granted. Perhaps this is what the psalmist meant when he wrote:

> Lord, make me to know my end,
> And what is the extent of my days,
> Let me know how transient I am (39:4).

Second, despite our need to perceive the measure of our days on earth, we must see that such realization often sends us through periods of destabilization. None of us faces our own death calmly. We may appear composed. But there is panic inside. Even our Lord was reduced to extreme anxiety when he confronted his impending arrest in the Garden of Gethsemane. As Mark so poignantly reports (14:33–34), Jesus

> *began to be very distressed and troubled. And He said to them, "My soul is deeply grieved to the point of death."*

To comprehend that we are going to die often makes us want to seek desperate avenues of escape. Once again, even our Lord was prompted to pray three times that the cup of death might pass from Him. Yet, unlike our Lord, many of us not only pray for the cup to pass, but we rush from the garden in frenzied retreat, taking whatever path of least resistance that we might encounter.

In recent years, the term "mid-life crisis" has become a household word. The phrase is used to explain a whole host of "destabilizing behaviors," to use a psychological phrase, often evidenced by adults in the midst of life. I am convinced, as are many, that the major cause of such reactionary behavior—affairs, divorce, drastic vocational changes, personality alterations—is the realization that life is half over, that the peak of the hill has been reached and the future is a downward spiral, that death is fast upon us. With a knee-jerk reaction, we rush out to be young again and grab all the gusto we can. In short, we often make some very serious and foolish mistakes. After all, a drowning man will grab hold of anything.

A perfect biblical example of this is found in the Old Testament character of Esau. It seems that Esau, the oldest son and principal heir of Isaac, was a gregarious man of the outdoors. He enjoyed farming and hunting. Once he was engaged in an extensive hunting trip for so long that he truly feared he might die of starvation. At last he was able to stumble home to find his conniving brother, Jacob, cooking a ravishing stew in the yard. The writer of Genesis describes the encounter in this way (25:29–34):

> And when Jacob had cooked stew, Esau came in from the field and he was famished; and Esau said to Jacob, "Please let me have a swallow of that red stuff there, for I am famished." Therefore his name was called Edom [meaning "the red"]. But Jacob said, "First sell me your birthright." And Esau said, "Behold, I am about to die; so of what use then is the birthright to me?" And Jacob said, "First swear to me"; so he swore to him, and sold his birthright to Jacob. Then Jacob gave Esau bread and lentil stew; and he ate and drank, and rose and went on his way. Then Esau despised his birthright.

So many people, like Esau, hear death rattling at their door and, in a moment of poor judgment, sell the birthright to all that is theirs. Like my grandfather drinking the soup of sexual lust, they lose their children, their marriage, their home, their vocation, their self-respect—all the things they have worked a lifetime to achieve. With Esau, they despise their birthright.

An encounter with death in the midst of life can, as in the case of Michener, kick us into a level of more productive and joyous living. But that same encounter can paradoxically cause us to be vulnerable to dreadful mistakes, to succumbing to poor judgment, to selling our birthright for a bowl of tepid stew.

When we become famished inside and are tempted to say with Esau, "Behold, I am about to die; so of what use then is the birthright to me?" we must somehow hold on and know that we are vulnerable to making disastrous decisions. We should try to delay major changes until we have gained some sense of stability again. Had Esau allowed himself fifteen minutes to sit quietly and chew on a piece of bread from his father's kitchen, he would have laughed at his brother's stinking stew and silly proposition. We, too, must recognize our vulnerability and, with God's strength, hold on until our equilibrium returns again.

And yet the question comes, in the heat of the night when passion is high and judgment is poor, how can we keep from selling our birthright? How can we hold on? Perhaps we can gain some insight from the life of Jesus.

As the night came when death rattled at Jesus' door, He recognized his vulnerability. He did not want to die. Consequently, He sought the strength of prayer in the garden of Gethsemane. We must not discount the place of prayer in Jesus' life. Prayer put Jesus in touch with the Spirit of God who empowered Him. Jesus was as strong as His prayer life was vital. We are no different from our Lord in that respect. In time of weakness, fear, and temptation we, too, must seek the stabilizing power of prayer.

Jesus, however, did more than pray. He also gathered His three closest friends about Him. As Mark recorded in his Gospel some thirty-five years after the events, when Jesus went to the garden of Gethsemane,

> *He took with Him Peter and James and John, and began to be very distressed and troubled. And he said to them, "My soul is deeply grieved to the point of death; remain here and keep watch"* (14:33–34).

Very forthrightly Jesus told his friends that he was struggling, that he was vulnerable and weak, that the prospect of death was unnerving him. Jesus asked them to *"remain here and keep watch."* Why? To warn Him of the approaching temple guard? No, I don't believe so. Rather, I think that Jesus was saying, "Brothers, keep an eye on Me. Strengthen Me with your presence. I was born for this moment. Don't let Me forsake it all now. Keep watch on Me." Tragically, the disciples fell asleep. But even the closeness of their slumbering bodies gave Jesus a warmth that helped melt the paralyzing chill of death.

No man or woman should face death alone, even death in the midst of life. Very often in the initial years of my ministry I felt so helpless, so useless standing by the hospital beds of patients in the waning moments of life. Doctors could order medication. Nurses could wipe their fevered brows. I just stood there feeling unskilled. However, I have come to see that when men and women confront death, what they need more than anything else is the presence of trusted friends. It is the comfort of human presence that blunts the sting of death.

When you feel death come upon you in the midst of life, do not struggle alone. Confide your struggle to your spouse. Talk with a few trusted friends. Seek the companionship of your pastor. The wolf likes to attack lone sheep. He veers away from the flock and shepherd. So ask others to "keep watch" with you. If they love you, they will be more than glad to see you through your night of instability and your moment of great promise. Indeed, they will allow you in turn to keep watch over them in the crises of their lives.

ⅢⅢ REFLECTIONS ⅢⅢ

And the Lord God planted a garden toward the east, in Eden; and there He placed the man whom He had formed. And out of the ground the Lord God caused to grow every tree that is pleasing to the sight and good for food; the tree of life also in the midst of the garden, and the tree of the knowledge of good and evil.

. . . And the Lord God commanded the man, saying, "From any tree of the garden you may eat freely; but from the tree of the knowledge of good and evil you shall not eat, for in the day that you eat from it you shall surely die."

. . . Now the serpent was more crafty than any beast of the field which the Lord God had made. And he said to the woman, "Indeed, has God said, 'You shall not eat from any tree of the garden'?" And the woman said to the serpent, "From the

fruit of the trees of the garden we may eat; but from the fruit of the tree which is in the middle of the garden, God has said, 'You shall not eat from it or touch it, lest you die'." And the serpent said to the woman, "You surely shall not die! For God knows that in the day you eat from it your eyes will be opened, and you will be like God, knowing good and evil." When the woman saw that the tree was good for food, and that it was a delight to the eyes, and that the tree was desirable to make one wise, she took from its fruit and ate; and she gave also to her husband with her, and he ate. Then the eyes of both of them were opened, and they knew that they were naked.

Genesis 2:8–9, 16–17; 3:1–7

Even though I walk through the valley of the shadow of death, I fear no evil; for Thou art with me; Thy rod and Thy staff, they comfort me.

Psalm 23:4

So teach us to number our days, That we may present to Thee a heart of wisdom.

Psalm 90:12

"And do not fear those who kill the body, but are unable to kill the soul; but rather fear Him who is able to destroy both soul and body in hell."

Matthew 10:28

"I do not ask Thee to take them out of the world, but to keep them from the evil one."

John 17:15

For I am already being poured out as a drink offering, and the time of my departure has come. I have fought the good fight, I have finished the course, I have kept the faith.

2 Timothy 4:6–7

Some people are so afraid to die that they never begin to live.

Henry van Dyke[2]

The fear of death is worse than death.

Robert Burton[3]

DEAR LORD:

I feel death's cold breath upon my neck, bearing down on me. I want to run, to flee, to escape into the embrace of the Tempter. O Father, keep watch with me.

As I kneel in my Gethsemane, provide me friends to comfort me. Give me the courage to openly say to them, "My soul is deeply grieved to the point of death." And through confession of fear and human frailty, may my confidence be restored to me.

Be Thou my Shepherd who comforts me even when "I walk through the valley of the shadow of death."

AMEN

15

THE GOD WHO WEEPS WITH US

A woman came to my office recently doubled over in the agony of grief. The week before, her only sister had died after a long and agonizing bout with lung cancer. At first, she tried to talk to me, to transform her feelings into words. Then she did the most honest thing she could do—she began to weep. For several minutes only her heaving sobs broke the silence. And then she managed to blurt between clinched teeth, "Scott, she was such a good woman. A great Christian. How could God let her die like that? How could He let her suffer so?"

The intensity of her statement was so electric, the flash in her eyes so vivid, that I was jolted. And then something broke loose inside me. I became a teenager again, hearing a rather sanctimonious lady who meant well say to me after my father's funeral, "He was so young, so talented—God must have had a very good reason for taking him." I spent years struggling with her statement, trying to understand how God could will my father's death—or anyone's death. Finally, I woke up one day and said, "She's wrong! She's absolutely wrong! God did not want my father to die. It just happened."

Perhaps one of the most difficult tasks I have as a minister is to tolerate some of the profane theology that floats around funeral parlors and in the homes of the bereaved. In these settings a loving God becomes one who takes children because He is "lonely," "wills" head-on collisions, and has "good reasons" for allowing a mother of four children to die. Sometimes I want to scream, "God had nothing to do with it! God is as grieved as you are!"

Recently, I read a very moving sermon by Dr. William Sloane Coffin, Jr., the senior minister of Riverside Church in New York City. The sermon was delivered ten days after Dr. Coffin's twenty-four-year-old son, Alex, died when his car skidded into Boston Harbor. Struggling with his own intense pain, Coffin bravely and lovingly faced his congregation and told them about an encounter he had had with a person who had come to comfort him by assuring him that Alex's death was within the "will of God." Exploding, Coffin had said to this would-be comforter:

> Do you think it was the will of God that Alex never fixed that lousy windshield wiper of his, that he was probably driving too fast in such a storm, that he probably had had a couple of "frosties" too many? Do you think that it is God's will that there are no streetlights along that stretch of road, and no guard rail separating the road and Boston Harbor?

And then Coffin said to his congregation:

> For some reason, nothing so infuriates me as the incapacity of seemingly intelligent people to get it through their heads that God doesn't go around this world with his fingers on triggers, his fist around knives, his hands on steering wheels. God is dead set against all unnatural death.[1]

Such well-meaning theology infuriates me, too. I confess that my knowledge of God is quite limited. But what I do know is that a God of love does not will sorrow, suffering, and death. How, then, can we reconcile our belief in a loving Father and the massive suffering in our world? I believe that a response to this dilemma must be approached from three perspectives.

First, I believe that God created and operates within the bounds of natural law. When a man falls over dead with a heart attack, it is not God who caused the heart attack but

rather natural law. Natural law dictates that too much cho-
lesterol in one's blood system, too little exercise, and exces-
sive stress will combine over a period of time to result in a
heart attack. Likewise, it is natural law that enables cancer
cells to multiply. It is natural law that causes an automobile
being driven too fast to slide out of control and crash into a
tree. God did not will the heart attack, or the cancer, or the
traffic fatality. But because of natural law and human nature,
the deaths occurred.

Yet people who will attribute an apple falling from a tree to
the law of gravity will turn right around and deem a child
fatally falling from a window ledge an act of God. Such logic
is not only irrational; it slanders the nature of God.

Second, having spotlighted the place of natural law in the
unfolding of tragic events, however, we must ask where God
fits into the picture. Is God a loving but passive God who in
detachment allows sin and tragedy to run rampant in our
universe? No, I do not think so. And it is at this point that I
cling to perhaps the most foundational scriptural life-rail in
my life.

Toward the end of his life, after seeing and experiencing
countless situations of toil and tragedy, the apostle Paul wrote
to the Christians at Rome:

*And we know that God causes all things to work together
for good to those who love God, to those who are called
according to His purpose* (Romans 8:28).

These words were central in Paul's understanding of human
suffering. And they are a cornerstone in my own theology.

Paul is saying that while God does not cause nor will
human suffering and tragedy, He is a God who does *actively
work through* the tragic to bring about good. God is by nature
one who creates beauty and healing out of ruin and chaos. He
is the God of the impossible.

Perhaps an example of what I am talking about can be seen
in my own life. As I have said, my father's death was tragic.
God did not will for a man forty-six years old to die at the
peak of his ministry potential leaving a wife with two chil-

dren to raise. I believe that when natural law snuffed out his life, the first to weep was God. God was in anguish! But God began to work actively through tragedy to bring about good.

Without doubt, God took care of my family's needs. But more than taking care of us, He took the very essence of tragedy and began to use it for good. I will not speak for my mother and sister, but I know that God used my experience of grief and death to cause me to dig deeper for meaning in life. He used the sharp edge of tragedy to shape me, to prod me, to carve out a vacuum in my life that would cause me to seek answers. And as a result, I believe that by God's grace, my experience of tragedy continues to make me into a better person, a deeper person, a more empathetic person than I might have been otherwise. Indeed, the ripple effect of tragedy being turned into goodness is still expanding. For without my own baptism into tragedy, I doubt that this pencil would be moving across this page at this moment. Indeed, you and I would not be having our present dialogue. God does cause all things to work together for good.

However, the paramount example of how God works through evil to bring about good is seen in the death and resurrection of Jesus Christ. I do not believe that God, like some cosmic puppeteer, wrote the script and pulled the strings that caused the gruesome execution of Jesus. Rather, sinful human nature and natural law combined to murder Jesus. When Jesus Christ died, God wept bitterly.

Yet, even through the tears, God immediately began to work to transform tragedy into goodness. Indeed, once and for all time God broke through the boundaries of natural law to proclaim that goodness ultimately overcomes evil. In the resurrection of Jesus from the dead, the greatest symbol of Christianity is seen. For the resurrection symbolizes for us that although God does not will or want tragedy, he can, nevertheless, snatch tragedy out of the jaws of evil and turn defeat into victory. In the resurrection God was saying to us: "All may seem hopeless, but I can take the shredded threads of despair and weave from them the strong fabric of victory. All may seem senseless tragedy, but if you will be patient, through time I will transform absurdity into meaningfulness;

pain into joy; tears into laughter; and separation into unity. All things will work together for good!''

But now let's leave the lofty clouds of theology and symbolism and get back to where you and I live. God did not interrupt natural law to raise William Sloane Coffin's son, or my father, or your loved one from the grave three days after they were buried. Although in faith we know they are with Him, we live in the gripping pain of their absence. So how can we begin to see our tragedy changed into goodness?

Returning to Paul's writing, we read that *"God causes all things to work together for good to those who love God, to those who are called according to his purpose."* In essence, we must see that we have a part to play in this transforming process as well. In order for God to work things together for good, he needs to work *through* men and women who (a) *love God,* and (b) have consciously responded to His *call* to achieve His *purpose* upon this earth. In other words, God needs *you*—your energy and love—to help Him change the tragedy of the death of a loved one into a resurrection of goodness.

I think again of the woman who visited my office after the death of her sister. Although overcome by grief, she has an opportunity to let God work through her to bring some good things out of tragedy. Her sister left two teenage daughters. Those girls need someone to love them, someone who instead of being bitter can say to them, "Girls, God didn't want your mother to die. In fact, He is weeping with us. God loves you very much. And I love you very much, too. I can't be your mother. I can't take her place. But we can have a really special relationship. We can get through this thing together." By letting God's love flow through her, this woman can allow God to begin to work through tragedy to bring about some very good things.

As I write the concluding lines to this chapter, I feel a sense of frustration that, in the face of human tragedy, simple and easy answers elude us all. Fully comprehending the mystery of a loving God working to bring about good in a world saturated with tragedy is impossible. But in the midst of mystery, of two things I am sure. God does not cause suffering and pain. And this same God of creation will, over the course of human history, take a great deal of evil and transform it into good. Clinging to this foundational belief, I, too, must say with Paul:

> For now we see in a mirror dimly, but then face to face; now I know in part, but then I shall know fully just as I have been fully known (1 Corinthians 13:12).

ⅢⅭⅫ REFLECTIONS ⅭⅫ

The Lord is near to the brokenhearted,
And saves those who are crushed in spirit.

Psalm 34:18

So when Jesus came, He found that [Lazarus] had already been in the tomb four days. . . . When Jesus therefore saw her [Mary] weeping, and the Jews who came with her, also weeping, He was deeply moved in spirit, and was troubled and said, "Where have you laid him?" They said to Him, "Lord, come and see." Jesus wept.

John 11:17, 33–35

Jesus said to her, "I am the resurrection and the life; he who believes in Me shall live even if he dies."

John 11:25

. . . for if we live, we live for the Lord, or if we die, we die for the Lord; therefore whether we live or die, we are the Lord's.

Romans 14:8

. . . that through death He might render powerless him who had the power of death, that is, the devil; and might deliver those who through fear of death were subject to slavery all their lives.

Hebrews 2:14–15

[God] shall wipe away every tear from their eyes; and there shall no longer be any death; there shall no longer be any mourning, or crying, or pain.

Revelation 21:4

There are wounds of the spirit which never close, and are intended in God's mercy to bring us ever nearer to Him, and to prevent us leaving Him by their very perpetuity. . . . This is how I comfort myself in my own great bereavements.

John Henry Newman[2]

If we could read the secret history of our enemies, we should find in each man's life sorrow and suffering enough to disarm all hostility.

Henry Wadsworth Longfellow[3]

Death be not proud, though some have called thee
Mighty and dreadful, for thou art not so;
For those, whom thou think'st thou dost overthrow
Die not, poor Death; nor yet canst thou kill me.
. . .
One short sleep past, we wake eternally,
And Death shall be no more: Death, thou shalt die!

John Donne[4]

Earth has no sorrow that Heaven cannot heal.

Thomas Moore[5]

Whoever is spared personal pain must feel himself called to help in diminishing the pain of others. We must all carry our share of misery which lies upon the world.

Albert Schweitzer[6]

We give back to you, O God, those whom you gave to us. You did not lose them when you gave them to us, and we do not lose them by their return to you. Your dear Son has taught us that life is eternal and love cannot die. So death is only an horizon and an horizon is only the limit of our sight.

William Penn[7]

DEAR FATHER:

In the midst of my grief, help me to know that You are weeping with me—that somehow my tears and Your tears will merge together to wash away bitterness and sorrow and despair. I know that You are a loving God, O Father, and regardless of circumstances, I cling to my faith in Your eternal goodness.

With Saint Francis of Assisi, I pray that You will make me an instrument of Your peace. May I be a source of comfort to the afflicted, a shoulder to weep on in the night, a friend who will dependably be there until the sun breaks forth again.

AMEN

16

LIVING WITH PARADOX

I was born in 1950, a "baby boom" child. Over the last forty years, my gregarious and outspoken generation has been known for many things—a glut in the school systems, televisionitis, the Peace Corps, the hippies, Vietnam, the sexual revolution, you name it. However, my generation and mine alone share one distinction that cannot be claimed by any other generation the world has known. We, the baby-boomers, are the first group of men and women to grow up knowing all of our lives that the insane touch of a button can wipe out the entire human race. With the advent of a mushroom cloud rising over Hiroshima in 1945, all of human history radically changed.

Having said this, however, I don't believe that the terrifying reality of nuclear war fully registered with me until 1973. All through the late 1960s and early 1970s, I had worried about being drafted and being sent to the quagmire of Vietnam. I had thought of death—my death—but never had I given serious reflection to the possibility that Vietnam might result in the massive destruction of a nuclear holocaust. With sorrowful relief, I watched the last of the American troops leave Vietnam and, like thousands of my peers, resolved to get on with life and look toward the future.

And then it happened. In October of 1973, all the world was caught off guard as Egyptian tanks crashed across the Sinai peninsula with lightning speed. The Israeli defense forces reeled back in disarray, and it seemed that nothing short of a military miracle would keep the walls of Jerusalem from falling once again. The State of Israel was facing imminent collapse. Suddenly it hit me: "Israel has the bomb! O God, Israel has the bomb! And faced with her own destruction, she will use it!" For the first time reality struck home—it is very possible for our world to be plunged into a suicidal nuclear conflict.

As Paul Harvey says, we know "the rest of the story." Israel successfully counterattacked with conventional weapons and a nuclear war was averted. But it could have happened. And, with that same blinding speed, the buttons could be pushed today. We live in a world teetering on the brink of insanity.

How crazy have things gotten? I was watching a television show recently that focused on the complex problems of nuclear disarmament. After twenty minutes of hearing experts and Pentagon officials wrangle about statistics and figures coded in a technological language I do not understand, my mind began to grow numb. Then the well-known astronomer, Carl Sagan, was interviewed. With an ironic smile he said, "Let's forget about all the numbers and megatons. Our world situation is like two mortal enemies finding themselves imprisoned and face to face inside a basement awash with gasoline. Menacingly, one man yells at the other, 'I have seventy matches and if you come one step farther, I'll strike one.' Replying to this threat, the other man screams across the darkness, 'Well, I have fifty matches and I'll strike two!' "[1] Sagan's point is well taken. One match or a hundred, it only takes a spark to ignite our world into a nuclear conflagration that will incinerate everyone.

And yet, although no one—Russian or American—would in their right mind launch a nuclear attack for offensive reasons, even the thought of nuclear weapons being used strictly for a defensive deterrent defies reason. As Frederick Buechner so cogently states:

The question is, what are we defending, our enemies and we? Well, we are defending our cities and towns. We are defending our homes, our children. We are defending the welfare of our people and the tradition of our fathers. And so of course are they. The tragic irony, of course, is that these precious things we and our enemies are both defending are threatened by nothing so much as by the very process we use to defend them.[2]

We live in the irony of the absurd. We threaten to strike a match in a room filled with gasoline in order to defend ourselves! You and I know this is crazy. But more than being ludicrous, the threat of nuclear holocaust constitutes the greatest ethical and moral issue our world has ever known. And baby-boomers who have come of age are going to have to eradicate this threat or be "boomed" off this earth.

How can we live emotionally healthy and positive lives given our grim global set of circumstances? Already nationwide surveys indicate that teenagers reflect an unhealthy anxiety level due to the specter of nuclear war. Indeed, when they think of the future, there is always a big question mark before their eyes as to whether there will be a future. So how can we emotionally cope with such threat and uncertainty?

In my own life, I have been greatly aided by reflecting on the writings of the Quaker minister Thomas R. Kelly. In his classic work *A Testament of Devotion* he writes:

> Ponder this paradox in religious experience: "Nothing matters; everything matters." . . . It is a key of entrance into suffering. He who knows only one-half of the paradox can never enter that door of mystery and survive.[3]

By looking at the two sides of this paradox, perhaps a sensible and stabilizing approach can be found to living with the constant threat of extinction.

First, let us look at the statement "everything matters." Very simply, this means that we must take ourselves and the world very seriously and say "it all matters." We must be Christian people who feel an ethical mandate to take action to reduce the threat of nuclear war. We must be individuals who refuse to say, "The problem is so big that I can't do anything about it." We must be activists who look our elected political officials in the eye and say, "Nuclear war matters to me! And it must matter to you!"

Edmund Burke once said, "The only thing necessary for the triumph of evil is for good men to do nothing."[4] Burke is absolutely correct. Martin Luther King, Jr., expressed the same thought in another fashion: "We can no longer lend our cooperation to an evil system. For he who accepts evil without protesting against it is really cooperating with evil."[5] As Christians, we must come to our senses and see that if we do not take aggressive and demonstrable action to safeguard our world from nuclear destruction, then when the buttons are pushed, *our* fingers will be doing the pushing.

And so you say, "What can I do?" Some of the options are obvious. You can work to influence our politicians. You can write your representatives in Congress. You can work within your denomination to see that nuclear war is viewed as a pressing ethical concern. And yet all these things I mention seem so mundane, so ineffective, so "much of the same."

Perhaps what we really need to do is to remember our Christian distinctive. We must recall the words of Jesus when he said:

> *"You are the salt of the earth. . . . You are the light of the world."*
> *"The kingdom of Heaven is like leaven"* (Matthew 5:13–14; 13:33).

In other words our role is to be the salt in human wounds that burns and heals, the light that reveals evil, the leaven that permeates slowly but surely through all the world and acts like a change agent. We must be a people who help others have an *attitudinal change* that causes them to say, "It matters! Everything matters!"

Reflecting on the importance of attitude in relationship to peace, the late Dr. William Barclay wrote:

> There can be no peace-making in the wrong atmosphere. If men have come together to hate, they will hate. If men have come together to refuse to understand, they will

misunderstand. If men have come together to see no other point of view but their own, they will see no other. But if men have come together, loving Christ and seeking to love each other, even those who are most widely separated can come together in love.[6]

Our task is by dogged and determined action to cast a light on the danger of nuclear war and to sow the mustard seed of love and compassion. Once again Christians are individually and collectively called upon to be the conscience of our society, the heart of the world, the leaven in the loaf.

Yet there is another side to the paradox. For while we are called to act and to say "everything matters," we must not forget that "nothing matters."

Though I am idealistic by nature, I have also lived long enough to develop my share of cynicism. I have preached numerous sermons on the perils of nuclear war. I have signed petitions, organized Peace Sunday observances, written resolutions, and attended peace conferences. But every time I shout "It matters!" I sadly remember a parable told by Sören Kierkegaard about a congregation of geese.

It seems that every Sunday the geese would waddle down to their church. The goose choir would process in, and the goose preacher would stand in the pulpit. Every Sunday the reverend gander would preach from the same text. Reading from Isaiah 40:31 he would proclaim, "Geese, God has given us wings. And with wings we can mount up like eagles and fly. We can soar in the sky. Nothing can confine us." And all the geese would quack "Amen!" and waddle home.[7]

The point is clear. How easy it is to talk about the dangers of nuclear war and yet little changes. How easy it is to grow discouraged, to be overcome by the massiveness of the problem we face and despair. It is in these moments when we must say, "Nothing matters."

What is meant by these terse words "nothing matters?" Very simply, but nonfatalistically, it means to say that "God is in charge of history, and He is big enough to handle it." It means that Someone bigger than we are is working with us on the problem, and we don't have to win the war by ourselves.

During the closing days of World War II the young German theologian Dietrich Bonhoeffer was implicated in a plot to assassinate Hitler and was thrown into prison. Knowing that millions of Jews were being murdered, that his country was being destroyed, and that the executioner's noose awaited him at any moment, he understandably began to despair. During this time, he wrote a poignant piece entitled "Who Am I?" One line in his composition, almost hidden amidst the existential richness of its surroundings, has been branded upon my memory. Confessionally speaking of his despair, Bonhoeffer asks:

Is something within me still like a beaten army, fleeing in disorder from a victory already achieved?[8]

These are words we need to ponder.

Bonhoeffer is intimating what I firmly believe—that God, the Lord of history, is already at the end of history. The victory has already been achieved. Now this does not release us who are Christians from responsibility. God is depending upon us to say "it matters" and to bring history toward victory. But we must see with Bonhoeffer that victory over sin, evil, and death has already been won and we must not retreat in despair.

As I look toward the future, I do not know whether nuclear war will kill us all. On the other hand, I do not know whether we will come to our senses and hammer our swords into plowshares, and our spears into pruning hooks. But either way, God will work through history to bring us back into union with Himself. And because of this faith, we can say "nothing matters."

In facing the future with all of its tentativeness and uncertainty, Christians in a nuclear age must learn to live with paradox. On the one hand, we must actively shout, "Everything matters!" and work like men and women possessed by the Spirit of God to bring peace to our world. On the other hand, we must be able to say deep within our souls "Nothing matters" and entrust the future to God. With Thomas Kelly we must realize that this paradox "is the key of entrance into suffering. He who knows only one-half of the paradox can never enter the door of mystery and survive.''

IIIᵉᴣ REFLECTIONS ᴄᴣIII

God is our refuge and strength,
A very present help in trouble.
Therefore we will not fear, though the earth should change,
And though the mountains slip into the heart of the sea;
Though its waters roar and foam
Though the mountains quake at its swelling pride.

                                        Psalm 46:1–3

And He will judge between the nations,
And will render decisions for many peoples;
And they will hammer their swords into plowshares, and
*   their spears into pruning hooks.*
Nation will not lift up sword against nation,
And never again will they learn war.

                                        Isaiah 2:4

Blessed are the peacemakers.

                                        Matthew 5:9

''These things I have spoken to you, that in Me you may have peace. In the world you will have tribulation, but take courage; I have overcome the world.''

                                        John 16:33

Who shall separate us from the love of Christ? Shall tribulation, or distress, or persecution, or famine, or nakedness, or peril, or sword? . . . But in all these things we overwhelmingly conquer through Him who loved us. For I am convinced that neither death, nor life, nor angels, nor principalities, nor things present, nor things to come, nor powers, nor height, nor depth, nor any other created thing, shall be able to separate us from the love of God, which is in Christ Jesus our Lord.

Romans 8:35, 37–39

So then let us pursue the things which make for peace and the building up of one another.

Romans 14:19

The world will never have lasting peace so long as men reserve for war the finest human qualities. Peace, no less than war, requires idealism and self-sacrifice and a righteous and dynamic faith.

John Foster Dulles[9]

Peace is what all desire, but all do not care for the things that pertain unto true peace.

Thomas à Kempis[10]

The "just" war principle is no longer feasible, for no atomic war can be just in either intention or conduct.

Henlee Barnett[11]

Peace cannot be kept by force. It can only be achieved by understanding.

Albert Einstein[12]

In modern warfare there are no victors; there are only survivors.

Lyndon B. Johnson[13]

The truly religious man does everything as if everything depended upon himself, and then leaves everything as if everything depended on God.

Joseph Parker[14]

DEAR FATHER:

When I was a child, I thought as a child, I believed that every question had an answer. And furthermore, every answer was an either/or proposition. Either the answer was right or wrong. Either the answer was black or white. Either the answer was good or bad.

But now, O Father, I am becoming an adult and am attempting to put away childish things. And in that process I am coming to see that the greatest truths in life are not either/or but rather are shrouded in the mystery of paradox.

O God, grant unto me the maturity to live in faith with the perplexity of paradox. May I deeply grasp the truth that in life everything matters and nothing matters. May I see that to be first I must be last, that to live I must die, that to be happy I must mourn, that to be at war with evil I must live in peace.

Father, in a world filled with paradox, may I hold firmly to the one thing that is absolute—Your eternal goodness.

AMEN

NOTES

1 STRENGTHENED BY FIRE

1. Ernest Hemingway, *A Farewell to Arms* (New York: Scribners, 1929), p. 249.
2. Henry Wadsworth Longfellow, *Hyperion: A Romance*, Longfellow's Prose Works, II (Boston: Houghton, Mifflin, 1895), p. 140.
3. Charles Spurgeon, quoted in Carrol E. Simcox, *A Treasury of Quotations on Christian Themes* (New York: The Seabury Press, 1975), p. 163.

2 FLOWERS THAT BLOOM

1. Thomas Merton, *Life and Holiness*, (New York: Doubleday, Image Books).
2. Alfred Delp, *The Prison Meditations* (New York: Macmillan, 1963), p. 84.

3 NO TRIALS SHALL OVERCOME YOU

1. Elton Trueblood, *Confronting Christ* (Waco, TX: Word Books, 1960), p. 9.
2. Dotson Nelson, a sermon delivered at First Baptist Church, Athens, GA., 1982.

4 A LIGHT IN THE DARKNESS

1. Paul Tournier, *The Meaning of Persons* (New York: Harper & Row, 1971), p. 17.

2. James Baldwin, source unknown.

3. Eddie Rickenbacker, quoted in Simcox, *A Treasury of Quotations on Christian Themes*, p. 163.

4. Eleanor Roosevelt, *You Can Learn by Loving* (New York: Harper & Row, 1960).

5. Albert Schweitzer, quoted in Michael E. McGill, *The Forty to Sixty Year Old Male* (New York: Simon & Schuster, 1980), p. 12.

5 A BECKONING DISTANCE

1. Erich Fromm, *The Art of Loving* (New York: Harper & Row, 1956), pp. 8–9.

2. Ibid.

3. Jess Lair, *I Ain't Much, Baby, But I'm All I've Got* (Garden City, NY: Doubleday & Co., 1969), p. 148.

4. George E. Vaillant, *Adaptation to Life* (Boston: Little, Brown and Co., 1977) p. 269.

5. Daniel Levinson, lecture given at Georgia State University, September 9, 1980.

6. Thomas Wolfe, "God's Lonely Man," in *The Hills Beyond* (New York: Harper & Row, 1941), p. 186. See also Edward C. Aswell's "A Note on Thomas Wolfe" in ibid., p. 383.

7. Francis Bacon, "Of Friendship," *Essays*.

8. John Donne, *Devotions XII*.

9. Emil Brunner, *The Christian Doctrine of God* (Philadelphia: Westminster Press, 1950), 1:260.

10. Augustine of Hippo, *Confessions*, Book I.

11. Luke 9:58.

A FEAR OF FEAR

1. Geoffrey Moorhouse, *The Fearful Void* (Philadelphia: J. B. Lippincott, 1974), pp. 18–19.

2. John McGowan, "Weatherman Wrestled Fear," *USA Today*, October 11, 1985, p. 2A.

3. James A. Garfield, source unknown.

4. Franklin D. Roosevelt, "First Inaugural Address," March 4, 1933.

5. John Newton, "Amazing Grace."

6. Alan Paton, *Instrument of Thy Peace*, rev. ed. (New York: Seabury Press, 1982).

7 ONE STEP AT A TIME

1. Jean de la Bruyère, *Les Caractères*.

2. Samuel Johnson, quoted in Tryon Edwards, ed. *The New Dictionary of Thoughts,* rev. ed. (Bloomington, IL: Standard Publishers, 1957), p. 11.

3. George MacDonald, quoted in Simcox, p. 56.

4. Mary B. C. Slade, "Footsteps of Jesus," *Baptist Hymnal* (Nashville: Convention Press, 1975), p. 325.

8 SHOW THEM YOU CAN'T PLAY

1. F. W. Woolsey, Louisville *Courier-Journal Magazine,* quoted in *Readers Digest* (June 1982), p. 58.

2. Sören Kierkegaard, quoted in Rollo May, *Man's Search for Himself* (New York: Norton, 1953), p. x.

3. Samuel Johnson, *Rasselas.*

4. Victor Frankl, quoted in *Pulpit Helps,* December 1979, p. 13.

5. Sören Kierkegaard, *Journals,* 1850.

6. William Jennings Bryan, source unknown.

7. Hans Selye, *Stress Without Distress* (New York: Signet Books, 1974), p.79.

9 ALWAYS ON TIME

1. Segal's Law, source unknown.

2. Paul Tournier, *A Place for You* (New York: Harper & Row, 1968), p. 51.

3. Lance Morrow, quoted in "Daydreams of What You'd Rather Be," *Time* 119 (June 28, 1982):78.

10 THE GOD OF ANOTHER CHANCE

1. Thomas Merton, *Thoughts in Solitude* (New York: Doubleday, Image Books, 1956), p. 81.

2. Dag Hammarskjold, "Whitsunday, 1961," *Markings,* trans. Leif Sjoberg and W. H. Auden (New York: Alfred Knopf, 1964), p. 205.

3. Thomas R. Kelly, *A Testament of Devotion* (New York: Harper & Row, 1941), p. 61.

4. Thomas à Kempis, *The Imitation of Christ,* Book 4, ch. 15.

11 TWO QUARTS LOW

1. Jerry R. Day, *Dealing with Depression* (Nashville: Sunday School Board of the Southern Baptist Convention, 1981), p. 4.

2. Albert Camus, "Actuelles," January 6, 1960, trans. Justin O'Brien, *Lyrical and Critical Essays*, Vintage Books (New York: Random House, 1970).

12 BE ANGRY, BUT DO NOT SIN

1. Aristotle, *Nichomachean Ethics,* 1106. This is actually an adaptation of Aristotle's statement.

2. Francis Quarles, *Enchyridion,* Book II, no. 60 (1641), reprint ed. (New York: AMS Press, 1967), Vol. 1.

3. Thomas Fuller, "Of Anger," *Holy and Profane State*.

4. William Blake, "A Poison Tree," *Songs of Experience*.

5. Cesare Pavese, *This Business of Living: Diary 1935–1950,* quoted in *The Oxford Book of Aphorisms* (Oxford: University Press, 1983), p. 41.

13 LIVING IN BABYLON

1. Martin P. Seligman, *Psychology Today* 7 (June 1973): 43.

2. Often called "The Serenity Prayer," this has been adapted from a 1934 prayer by Reinhold Niebuhr: "O God, give us serenity to accept what cannot be changed, courage to change what should be changed, and wisdom to distinguish

the one from the other." It has been adopted as the prayer of Alcoholics Anonymous. June Bingham, *Courage to Change: An Introduction to the Life and Thought of Reinhold Niebuhr* (New York: 1961). See footnote to quotation in John Bartlett, *Familiar Quotations*, 14th ed. (Boston: Little, Brown, 1968), p. 1024.

14 DEATH IN THE MIDST OF LIFE

1. John P. Hayes, *James A. Michener: A Biography* (Indianapolis: Bobbs-Merrill, 1984), p. 65.
2. Henry Van Dyke, quoted in Frank S. Mead, *The Encyclopedia of Religious Quotations* (Old Tappan, NJ: Fleming H Revell, 1965), p. 145.
3. Robert Burton, *Anatomy of Melancholy*, Maxim 511.

15 THE GOD WHO WEEPS WITH US

1. William Sloane Coffin, "My Son Beat Me to the Grave," *Yankee*, December 1983, p. 168.
2. John Henry Newman, source unknown.
3. Henry Wadsworth Longfellow, *Drift-Wood*, Longfellow's Prose Works, I (Boston: Houghton Mifflin, 1895).
4. John Donne, "Death."
5. Thomas Moore, "Come Ye Disconsolate."
6. Albert Schweitzer, *Memoirs of Childhood and Youth*, p. 61, quoted in Erica Anderson, ed., *The World of Albert Schweitzer* (New York: Harper & Row, 1955), p. 11.
7. William Penn, quoted in George Appleton, ed., *The Oxford Book of Prayer* (Oxford: University Press, 1985), p. 163.

16 LIVING WITH PARADOX

1. The interview with Carl Sagan took place in 1985.
2. Frederick Buechner, *A Room Called Remember* (San Francisco: Harper & Row, 1984), p. 76.
3. Kelly, *A Testament of Devotion*, p. 68.
4. Edmund Burke, Letter to William Smith, January 9, 1795. Given in John Bartlett, *Familiar Quotations*, 15th ed. (Boston: Little, Brown, 1982), p. 454.

5. Stephen B. Oates, *Let the Trumpet Sound: The Life of Martin Luther King, Jr.* (New York: Plume, 1982), p. 66.

6. William Barclay, *The Gospel of Mark,* The Daily Study Bible Series (Philadelphia: Westminster, 1975), pp. 140–41.

7. Sören Kierkegaard, ''The Tame Geese,'' *The Journals of Sören Kierkegaard: A Selection,* ed. & trans. Alexander Dru (New York: Oxford, 1935), quoted in Robert Bretall, ed., *A Kierkegaard Anthology* (New York: Modern Library, 1959), p. 433.

8. Dietrich Bonhoeffer, *Letters and Papers from Prison,* trans. Eberhard Bethge (New York: The Macmillan Company, 1963), p. 347.

9. John Foster Dulles, quoted in Mead, *Encyclopedia of Religious Quotations,* p. 325.

10. à Kempis, *The Imitation of Christ,* Book 3, ch. 25.

11. Henlee Barnett, *Introducing Christian Ethics* (Nashville: Broadman Press, 1961), p. 171.

12. Albert Einstein, quoted in Simcox, *A Treasury of Quotations,* p. 200.

13. Lyndon B. Johnson, quoted in *ibid.,* p. 112.

14. Joseph Parker, quoted in Mead, *Encyclopedia of Religious Quotations,* p. 136.

About the Author

Scott Walker, the son of missionary parents, spent part of his childhood in the Philippines. He and his wife and their two sons live in South Carolina, where he is the pastor of First Baptist Church. He is also the author of *Where the Rivers Flow* and *Discovering Exodus*.

TA-63